$\mathcal{H}$EAL MY $\mathcal{H}$EART, $\mathcal{L}$ORD

EMILIE BARNES
with
ANNE CHRISTIAN BUCHANAN

HARVEST HOUSE PUBLISHERS

EUGENE, OREGON

Cover by Terry Dugan Design, Minneapolis, Minnesota

Cover photo © Jim Franco / Botanica / Getty Images

HEAL MY HEART, LORD
Copyright © 1996 by Harvest House Publishers, Inc.
Published by Harvest House Publishers
Eugene, Oregon 97402

Library of Congress Cataloging-in-Publication Data

Barnes, Emilie.
   Heal my heart, Lord / Emilie Barnes with Anne Christian Buchanan.
      p. cm.
   First work originally published: My cup overflows. Eugene, Or.: Harvest House Publishers, ©1998. 2nd work originally published: Fill my cup, Lord. Eugene, Or.: Harvest House Publishers, ©1996.
   Includes bibliographical references.
   ISBN-13: 978-0-7369-1606-6 (pbk.)
   ISBN-10: 0-7369-1606-7
   1. Consolation.   2. Bible. O.T. Psalms XXIII—Meditations.   3. Christian life—Meditations.   I. Buchanan, Anne Christian.   II. Barnes, Emilie. My cup overflows. III. Barnes, Emilie. Fill my cup, Lord.   IV. Title.
   BV4909.B375 2006
   242'.4—dc22   2005022275

Printed in the United States of America

07 08 09 10 11 12 13 14 / VP-MS / 10 9 8 7 6 5 4 3

Dedication

*To my daughter, Jenny, who loves
Christ from the top of her head to the
tips of her fingers to the bottom of her feet. You
are a joy to our family.*

*Without you, sweet one, this book
would have never been written.*

*I love you deeply and dearly.
Your forever Ma Ma*

Contents

A Word Before You Start

Every life is a journey. And for authors like me whose books grow out of their life, each book is a kind of snapshot, taken at a specific moment of the trip. So it's no surprise to look back at earlier books and discover some details are a little off. It's like looking at a photo of a memorable moment and realizing the hairstyles are out of date or your children have grown or that you no longer own that couch.

But what a joy to look back at an earlier "snapshot" and realize that, little differences or not, it's still a pretty good picture! The people you love are there. The baby's adorable. You always liked that couch. In the ways that really count, the snapshot still tells a true and valuable story.

I felt the same kind of joy when Harvest House asked me to look back over the two little books that make up this volume and decide whether to reissue them. They tell of things I learned about God during a period of great change in my life. And though my circumstances have changed quite a bit since they were written, they still seem to speak the truth as I see it.

When I wrote the first book, I was deeply involved

in a hectic career of writing books, speaking at nationwide seminars, and maintaining a lively mail-order business. I was needing to confront some painful issues from my past. And God was teaching me some valuable lessons about what it meant to come to him for strength and healing for my heart in the midst of my very busy life.

I needed that strength and healing even more acutely a few years later, when my busy life took a more painful turn. A family crisis and then a series of health problems pushed me to dig deeper into what it means to depend on God during those "rainy seasons" of life when the problems don't seem to stop.

As it turned out, the "rainy season" I described in the second book was really just the beginning of an incredible period in my life's journey—a time when almost everything seemed to change. I'll give a brief update at the end of this book to let you know how the story has turned out...so far.

But the interesting thing, I've discovered, is that these "snapshots" from the earlier part of my journey still depict something real and true. I still need strength for my busy life, still need help in confronting the past, still need comfort for my pain and healing for both body and soul. From my conversations with women across the country, I suspect you may need these things too.

The good news is: God is still God. Our hairstyles

and our furniture and our life circumstances may change, but God doesn't. He knows the end of the story from the beginning. And he is the One who can take your cup of stress…or resentment…or worry… or pain…and fill it to overflowing with comfort and strength. He is the One who can truly heal your heart.

So if there's anything true about the "snapshots" in this book, if they still hold up after almost a decade, it's really because God has been in the picture all the time. His story is always fresh, his mercies new every morning.

My prayer is always that, in reading my words, you'll catch a glimpse of his loving face.

Can You Fix This, Lord?

Can you fix this, Lord?
Will you fix this?
I need a bit of a miracle
Right about now.
I've got these broken relationships—
And these broken dreams,
And this broken heart.
I need you, Lord.
When I'm hurting,
What I need most of all
Is to be cradled
In your everlasting arms.
Can you fix this?
Will you fix this?

1

God Will Heal Your Heart

Create in me a pure heart, O God,
And renew a steadfast spirit within me.
Do not cast me from your presence or take
your Holy Spirit from me.
Restore to me the joy of your salvation
And grant me a willing spirit, to sustain me.
—PSALM 5:10-12 NIV

When my children (and later my grandchildren) were small, I used to delight in fixing things for them.

What a sense of satisfaction to be able to take a broken toy or a ripped shirt or a skinned knee and "make it all better" with a tube of glue or a spool of thread or a Band-Aid or just a kiss.

I also enjoyed immensely, in the days when I had a little more time and a lot less money, the process of restoring old, beat-up furniture or decorative items. With a little paint or varnish, a yard or two of fabric, and a little creative imagination, almost any worn-out item could be restored to beauty or usefulness.

I used to find such joy in my own small efforts at restoration.

So in the past few years, when I myself have felt so broken and worn, I've wondered if my heavenly Father finds the same kind of joy in restoring me.

For restoration is exactly what he promises us through Scripture.

"He restores my soul," sings the psalmist.

"The God of all grace, who has called you to his eternal glory in Christ, will himself restore...you," says Peter.

In the Old Testament, God repeatedly promised his people through the prophets that he would restore the health of their nation.

Jesus, throughout his earthly ministry, restored physical health, spiritual health, even physical life... and passed that restorative power on to his followers through the Holy Spirit.

Even the biblical depictions of the end times are a magnificent epic of restoration, a promise to bring about a new heaven and a new earth—all fixed, redeemed, and shining good as new.

Magnificently "all better."

And that, of course, is what we all long for, especially in the rainy seasons of our lives.

When illness strikes, when experiences knock

us low, when life leaves us wounded, our natural heart-cry to our heavenly Father is the cry of a child: "Please make it all better."

And he does just that. I believe it with all my heart.

God is using all our circumstances to bring us closer to him (and to each other), teaching us to rely on him for our healing and restoration. And he is teaching me a lot about what it really means to be healed and restored.

I am learning, for instance, that my healing is intended to be a partnership. God does the restoration, but I am not just a passive participant. I am expected to respond and participate in the process.

I participate in the healing of my body, for instance, by following what I believe to be God's plan for a healthy life: natural nutrition, enough water, adequate exercise, enough rest. I pray for healing, and I gratefully accept the prayers of others (just as I pray for them).

At the same time, I'm trying to participate in the healing of my own soul and spirit by keeping my heart open to God, learning more about how he works, and most of all by offering him my overflowing cup and asking him to purify and restore me.

This is another thing I am learning about the process of restoration. It has a lot to do with coming clean.

My current round of physical restoration began, I believe, with the process of flushing out the toxins from my body through a program of healthy nutrition. I took my body to my nutritional consultant and she helped me begin the process of cleaning and purifying my poisoned system.

I am absolutely convinced that my spiritual restoration, as well, depends on the process of ridding my soul of spiritual toxins: stress, bitterness, resentment, rebellion, unprocessed grief, distrust. In the Bible, healing is always tied in with forgiveness of sins and cleansing of life. And I think that is absolutely true for our lives as well.

In *Fill My Cup, Lord,* I pictured this process as one of emptying our cups of these dark substances and then surrendering those cups to the Lord to be wiped clean and filled with quietness, encouragement, and forgiveness.

In our seminars we illustrate this process even more graphically, with a huge black ceramic cappuccino cup. I fill the black cup with little slips of black paper to illustrate how our cups become full of dark attitudes and emotions and thoughts and beliefs, desperately in need of a good cleaning. I urge the women to take their "cup of darkness" to the foot of the cross and dump all the blackness at the feet of Jesus. (At that point I actually turn the black cup over and dump out all those little pieces of black paper.)

Then I hold up another big cup, the twin of the first, except that it's gleaming white. And I ask them to picture looking into their cups and seeing them shine with white purity—unstained and unsullied, beautiful and bright and clean.

It's a simple but profound illustration. The on-going and unending process in this life of becoming clean is one of the keys to being made "all better."

After one seminar, a woman came up to me and said, "You know, I dumped all the blackness out of my cup, and when I looked in I saw there was still something left. And I realized that I was still harboring some resentment in my heart that needs to be emptied. I'm going to go home and get my cup clean by asking forgiveness of someone."

That's exactly what we need to do to participate in our own restoration. We need to concentrate on keeping our cups clean, going to the Lord, emptying out our cups of darkness, asking to be purified and refilled. We need to stay close to him: reading the Scriptures, spending time in prayer, listening to his Word about what our part in our own healing will be.

And this is crucially important: We need to obey. Now, more than ever, I am convinced that a vital key to restoration is simply *not saying no* to God when we hear his voice.

A few years ago, I saw my daughter, Jenny,

floundering around, lashing out, confused about who she was and where she fit in her own life. The brokenness in our lives over Jenny's separation from her husband didn't begin to be repaired until I managed to hear God's Word about asking forgiveness and then, as hard as it was, to obey. I didn't really want to ask Jenny's forgiveness. I was still convinced she was the one in the wrong. But I didn't want to say no to God, so I did what he said. Since then I have watched with awe as Jenny has determined to participate in her own healing by obeying God. Today I see her praying with her children, doing what she can to help them in their own pain, reaching out to her friends and the people in her new neighborhood. I've seen her obey God when she really didn't want to, and the result has been phenomenal growth in her life.

So we do participate in our own restoration. Through ongoing surrender and obedience, even when it's hard, we help in the process of ridding our lives of physical and emotional and spiritual toxins that are poisoning our lives and preventing our healing and growth.

And yet there always comes a point when we reach the limits of our participation. At some point we have to come back to the realization that God, once again, is in charge of how we heal and when we heal and what the end result will be. He alone is the one who can ultimately "make it all better." But that is wonderful news to me, because only in him does "all better" mean perfect, fully whole, completely redeemed, remade, more beautiful than we ever imagined, with no seams, no scars, no Band-Aids, no patches.

It's a little like Margery Williams' beautiful little story of *The Velveteen Rabbit*. No doubt you have read this beloved children's book about the little stuffed rabbit who wanted to be real. This toy rabbit was loved by his young owner until his velveteen fur was worn and his face was gone and his stuffing was coming out. But somehow, in the process of being loved to tatters, this little toy bunny was given the gift of becoming "real."

The point of the story, of course, was that we become real by loving and being loved, but that in the process we get hurt and collect some scars.

But I think the ending of that beautiful little story makes another point as well.

In his first life the velveteen rabbit was a stuffed toy covered with scars.

By the end of the story, though, he was not just repaired. He wasn't just patched up, glued together, fixed up.

Instead, the velveteen rabbit was transformed, made new, still fully himself but at the same time fully new. He wasn't a patched-up toy bunny. He was a beautiful, bounding, real rabbit, set free by love to explore an entirely new world.

And that's the kind of healing I look forward to eventually, when I'm through with this life and ready for my new life in the Lord.

Here on earth, the restoration we experience is an ongoing process, truly miraculous but partial and problematic. Here on earth, the very process of healing leaves us inevitably marked and scarred (not to mention wrinkled and sagging).

In the end, though, the healing we are promised is full and complete. When God is through with us, we will be more real than we ever thought possible—as well as unscarred and unwrinkled and energetic and full of life and love.

I don't know about you, but I just can't wait!

Some Words for a Broken Heart

2 Kings 20:5
I have heard your prayer, I have seen your tears; surely I will heal you.

ACTS 28:27

For the hearts of this people have grown dull. Their ears are hard of hearing, and their eyes they have closed, lest they should see with their eyes and hear with their ears, lest they should understand with their hearts and turn, so that I should heal them.

PSALM 71:20-21

You, who have shown me great and severe troubles, shall revive me again, and bring me up again from the depths of the earth. You shall increase my greatness, and comfort me on every side.

DEUTERONOMY 4:29-31

But from there you will seek the LORD your God, and you will find Him if you seek Him with all your heart and with all your soul. When you are in distress, and all these things come upon you in the latter days, when you turn to the LORD your God and obey His voice (for the LORD your God is a merciful God), He will not forsake you nor destroy you.

I Wonder, Lord...

I find myself wondering, Lord,
How my life can be so full
And yet my heart and soul so thirsty.
Physically, emotionally, and spiritually
I am drained.
I need you to fill my cup, Lord.
I offer you the one I have filled with stress
And ask that you replace it
With one you have filled with quietness.

2

God Heals Busy Hearts

Be still, and know that I am God.
—PSALM 46:10

Quiet time.

It's a lovely phrase, isn't it? To me, "quiet time" summons up images of stillness and serenity, of a quiet communion with God on a beautiful garden patio or in a cozy window seat—reading his Word and praying and journaling while a fragrant cup of tea steams at my elbow.

And I have had wonderful quiet times like that.

But these days, I have to confess, my quiet times are not always so quiet—at least not at first. Sometimes they start out more like silent wrestling matches as I struggle with my fears, my worries, my pain.

Do you have times like that? Times when you seek out solitude, flee into stillness, only to find that your worries have followed and refuse to leave you alone? Or times when your schedule is so demanding that quiet time with God feels like just one more chore you can't manage?

If so, I have good news for you. A quiet spirit is not a requirement for a quiet time with the Lord.

Yes, I need to be willing to come to him, to offer him my cup filled with whatever is troubling me. But if I do that, I have found that he can supply the quiet spirit. If I can manage to hand over that cup of trouble, he can and will fill it to overflowing with serenity and peace.

What a wonderful thing to know, to remember, to remind yourself of when you feel overwhelmed with busyness or with pain. You don't have to come to him quiet. You just need to come to him.

The last few years have not been easy ones for our family. Not only has our schedule been packed with important but wearying obligations, but the trauma of an impending divorce has also torn a big rip in the fabric of our lives. I've had to watch as people I love make decisions I don't understand or approve of, and I've agonized as others I love suffer hurts I can't soothe. I've had to wait for answers and understanding and resolution that just haven't come yet.

That's why so many of my quiet times lately have started out anything but quiet. Often I have been angry or torn or worried or scared.

But that's why I need the quiet in the first place.

When my mind is full of clamor and my cup is full of trouble, that's when I most need to hear God's still small voice, and to feel his peace.

This is what I'm learning once again as I hold up my cup to the Lord and seek to spend time with him:

My quiet time is not a gift I give to God.

My quiet time is a gift God gives to me.

I don't offer him my quiet time. I simply offer him my time, my self. He's the one who provides the quiet spirit.

I come to him with my cup of confusion and worry. He's the one who takes that cup and empties it and then pours it full of quietness and peace.

He supplies the quiet. I supply the time.

That's one reason I can have quiet time, if necessary, in places that are not absolutely quiet. Quiet doesn't always require solitude. In fact, I've had some of my most meaningful quiet times on airplanes or in crowded restaurants, with engine noise buffeting my ears and people pressed in around me. My spirit was with the Lord, silently holding up my cup to him, and he provided the gift of quietness in the midst of a whirlwind.

But quietness does seem to require that I make the conscious effort to get away from the distractions of those who need me or who claim my attention. That's why I can have quiet time on a noisy airplane where no one knows me but not during a family dinner or on the floor of a conference where I am speaking. I need to pull away, to shut a door, to put space between me and the ordinary demands of my day. And in order for that to happen, I usually need to schedule my time for being with God.

But I don't need to "get quiet" in order to draw near to God. I just need to be willing to come to him.

Of course, it's wonderful to go to a place where physical quietness can help foster spiritual quietness. God has always spoken quieting words to me through his creation, so I love to have my quiet times out of doors. I love to go to a park, into a yard, under a tree—where I can see the butterfly flap its wings in spring or watch the colored leaves drift off the trees in fall. God works in my heart through nature, soothing my spirit with growing things and gentle breezes.

For several years now, my quiet times have tended to coincide with my morning walks. Yes, I love a quiet moment with a cup of tea, but I prefer company for tea. And yes, I have my daily times with my prayer notebook, when I try to be faithful to my prayer promises, interceding for my family and for my church and for those who have requested my prayers.

But when my cup is full of trouble and I really

need to be alone with God, I like to lace up my tennies and set out on the path along the long irrigation canal that runs through our town.

I know that two-mile course now like the back of my hand. I know where the rocks jut up, where the path grows narrow, where the orange blossoms smell the sweetest, where a recent rain will make a mud puddle on the path. I feel safe among the many other joggers and walkers (and their dogs) that use the path. And somehow the rhythm of my Reeboks on that familiar path helps me walk my thoughts toward my heavenly Father.

Because I know the route so well, I sometimes read as I walk—or read a bit and then walk a bit. I carry a little book of scriptural prayers, and I read a few and then let them work into my mind as I stride along. Over the past year or so, I've prayed through several of these books more than once (I write the date in the back cover when I finish one and start over).

But I don't wait until I feel spiritual to start walking. I simply put one foot in front of the other. As I walk I simply let my thoughts and feelings and confusions and stresses rise up in my mind, turning them over to God. And most of the time, by the time my forty-five-minute walk is over, the quiet has usually come.

Sometimes it takes awhile. Most days, in fact,

it takes at least twenty minutes for the noise and busyness of my everyday life to sift out of my head and for my internal strife to settle down. It seems to take that twenty minutes of walking to get my cup rinsed out and ready for the Lord's filling.

I may not be consciously praying or even thinking during that time. I'm simply walking and letting the breeze wash over me and listening to the birds sing and smelling the orange blossoms and letting the Scriptures or whatever else I've been reading speak to my spirit in the silence.

And then, in the last twenty minutes of my walk, something almost always happens. The "to dos" and "I've gottas" and "but what abouts" in my head begin to subside, and God's peace begins to settle into my spirit. And then, when I'm finally able to listen, God whispers his word of peace and comfort, or guidance and challenge.

Sometimes I remember a passage of Scripture. Sometimes a knotty problem seems to unravel itself in my head. Sometimes I am simply strengthened to go on with my life. Tears often flow—tears of relief and release as my cup of troubles is poured out and the quietness flows in to take its place.

No, it doesn't always take that long. I have found that if I offer to God whatever time I have, he honors that time. If I only have fifteen minutes but bring those fifteen minutes to him, he can give me what I need in those fifteen minutes. But, then the sweet taste of his peace leaves me wanting more and more.

And no, it doesn't happen every single time. It's not a cut-and-dried transaction: I come to God; he gives me peace. It's a relationship. The peace comes from spending time with the one who speaks in silence. The quietness comes from being with him and letting him rearrange my thought processes.

There have been a few times on the canal path (and on the patio and on the airplane) when nothing seems to change—when I have come to God agitated and gone away agitated. Sometimes in retrospect I can understand what happened. I was holding on too tightly to my troubles, unwilling to give up control even to God.

Or I needed to learn something or do some growing, and God was using my discomfort to motivate me. I don't know all the answers for those times when my quiet time never got quiet. God rarely works on my schedule, and sometimes my cup filled with peace more slowly than I expected.

But I have to tell you that those times have been rare, even in the difficult years. Almost always, I have come away from my quiet times with my cup overflowing. Again and again, when I gave the Lord my chaos, he has given me his peace.

More and more, that is what I am yearning to do.

The longer I live, the more I thirst for those quiet times in my heavenly Father's presence, the more I long to climb up into the lap of my Abba-Daddy and enjoy the security of those everlasting arms. Sometimes I feel like a toddler stretching my own arms up, dancing on my toes, begging to be held by the One who loves me so much.

"Up, Daddy. Want up."

And then he lifts me up.

The longer I live, the more I know that if I will just hold up my cup to him, even my cup of anger and stress and trouble and confusion, he will be faithful to fill my cup with the peace of his presence.

Some Words for a Busy Heart

JOB 34:29

When He gives quietness, who then can make trouble?

PSALM 23:2

He makes me to lie down in green pastures;
He leads me beside the still waters.

ECCLESIASTES 4:6

Better a handful with quietness than both
hands full, together with toil and grasping
for the wind.

ISAIAH 30:15

In returning and rest you shall be saved;
in quietness and confidence shall be your
strength.

PSALM 107:28-30

Then they cry out to the LORD in their
trouble, and He brings them out of their
distresses. He calms the storm, so that its
waves are still. Then they are glad because
they are quiet; so He guides them to their
desired haven.

You Know Best, Lord

You know best, Lord.
You are capable of running the universe
And I am not.
Sometimes I think I am able,
And I try to take back the controls to my life.
Sometimes I let myself get bogged down
With fear and worry and overcontrol.
Thank you for reminding me
That you already have everything planned out
As it should be.
Thank you for reminding me to
Trust in your sovereignty
And to wait on you.

3

God Heals Distrusting Hearts

The Lord is my strength and my shield;
My heart trusted in Him, and I am helped,
Therefore my heart greatly rejoices,
And with my song I will praise Him.
—PSALM 28:7

One day Bob and I were in our van, trying to cross a really busy highway. There was no traffic light at this particular intersection, and the cars were whizzing by right and left. Bob was craning his neck, trying to find an opening. I didn't want to add to his worries, so I just sat quietly.

We sat there for several minutes with Bob poised to make his move. Finally he saw his opening and zipped out across the road. We made it!

As we continued on our way, Bob looked over at me. "You know, Em, I noticed you weren't even looking at all those cars. Weren't you worried we wouldn't get across?"

"Oh," I said without thinking, "I trust you."

Bob's questioning expression turned into a beaming smile. "Thank you," he said.

I was a little surprised by his enthusiastic response. But when I thought about it a little more, I understood why he was so pleased.

You see, trust is a compliment. It's a gesture of respect, a gift of esteem. And it's a gift not lightly given, because trust is also a risk. Trusting someone means giving that person a little bit of control over our lives—which means that other person may let us down.

That's why the trust of a child is so poignant. When a little one reaches up and takes my hand, I feel a little tug at my heartstrings because I know she's giving me the gift of her trust. She's trusting that I will help her and not hurt her, that I will meet her needs. Then I feel a surge of responsibility, because I know just how vulnerable that little child is. And I also feel a little stab of pain because I know this world can be so untrustworthy.

"Hey, trust me." Can you even hear the words without feeling a tingle of distrust? These days it seems we're bombarded with all the bad things that can happen if we let down our guard and trust *anybody*. We can be bilked or conned. We can be cheated, mugged, even murdered.

And we don't even need to leave home to be let down. Anyone who has ever lived in a relationship knows that. A promise broken, a responsibility shirked, a word spoken or not spoken—friends and families can betray each other with devastating accuracy. We do it out of carelessness, out of cruelty, out of our own mistrust.

I can still taste the bitter cup of betrayal and disappointment and fear I drank as a young girl growing up with an alcoholic father. I knew that my daddy loved me, but I couldn't trust him to control himself, to be consistent with me. I couldn't even trust him to go on living. Daddy died when I was eleven—and to a child, the death of a parent feels like abandonment, the ultimate betrayal.

I also knew the agony of trust when one of my uncles violated my body. "Come sit with me," he would say, and when I obeyed he would begin fondling me. Eventually I would get up and leave the room. I don't know why I didn't kick or scream or tell my aunt—perhaps because I had been raised to obey all adults. But I still remember that deep sense of betrayal when someone I trusted hurt me.

But you don't need my stories to convince you it's an untrustworthy world. You have your own stories. You know what it is like to be betrayed by those to whom you gave the gift of your trust. And you know you have to "be careful out there."

And yet, not trusting is not an option—if we want to have any relationships at all. We can't be close to anyone without giving that person the gift of our trust. We have to take the risk, even when we know we could be hurt.

The crucial questions, of course, are who and how. Whom can I trust? And how can I manage to trust again when my trust has been betrayed?

When it comes to people, there aren't any guarantees. We can be wise when it comes to choosing the people we relate to, trusting in our own instincts and the counsel of others and the nudging of the Holy Spirit. We can follow some commonsense precautions—like letting relationships develop slowly and not giving credit card numbers to people who call—to keep from becoming involved with extremely untrustworthy people. But even those precautions can't keep us truly safe.

The trouble is that *everyone* is untrustworthy at one time or another. We *all* let each other down. So I think we need to look a little deeper when it comes to choosing whom and how we are going to trust.

When it comes to people, I think we need to look at character and intentions—and what we are trusting others to be and do.

You see, I do trust my husband, Bob. I trust him profoundly. And yet I don't trust him never to make a mistake. I don't trust him never to hurt my feelings or forget an appointment or utter an unkind word. I don't trust my Bob not to be human. If I did, I would be setting myself up for long-term disappointment and bitterness.

What I do trust is Bob's fundamental character. I trust him to be the kind and competent man I know him to be. I trust him to want to stay in relationship with me, to want the best for me. I trust him to learn from his mistakes and to continue to grow.

And how do I know what Bob's character is like and what his intentions are? He's shown me! Over and over again in our life together he has shown that he can be trusted. Even before I met him or knew him well, I knew him by reputation. Mutual friends assured me that he was "all right." I also believe the Holy Spirit was working in my heart, softening it and allowing me to trust in the man God had chosen for me.

All of this brings me to the issue of trusting God. And sometimes I think it's a lot harder for me to trust God than it is to trust an imperfect (but wonderful) human like Bob. After all, God is a spirit. I can't touch him or smell him or see him. Like most people, I have my moments when I doubt he even exists.

And yet I need to trust God if I am going to live in relationship with him. I need to trust God in order to trust anyone else—for how else can I have the security to give the gift of my trust to people I know might let me down?

So how can I trust God?

Basically, it works with God the way it works with Bob.

I trust God because of what he is like, because of what he has done. And I know these things both from my own experience and from what I have seen in the lives of others. I can trust God because he has shown me who he is and what his intentions are toward me and all his people. Over and over, by his Word and his actions, he has shown that he is a God who can be trusted.

The holy Scriptures give dramatic witness to God's trustworthiness. The psalmist and the prophets and the gospels say it in pictures. The Lord is my rock. He is my help and shield. He is my redeemer. He is the bread of life, the living water, the good shepherd, the way and the truth and the life.

The Scriptures say it in story, too. Once upon a time there was a God who created human beings and chose a specific group of people to belong to him and show him to the world. Over the centuries this God cared for his people and rescued them and disciplined them and persistently loved them even when they turned their backs on him. And then this God made the ultimate commitment, passed the ultimate test of character and intent. He sent his only Son to die for those people—to show us just how deeply he can be trusted.

To me the most incredible part in this whole

incredible scriptural story is that I'm part of it. I, too, am created and rescued and disciplined and loved and redeemed by God. I, too, have a part in God's story. And my part is, in essence, to trust him, to let him work in my life and change me and guide me.

This really is a God I can trust. He's shown me by what he has done in the lives of so many people I know. Again and again, in the face of pain and doubt and despair, my God has proved himself trustworthy—I've seen it happen.

I think of my friend Carol, who lost her beloved husband Bill 16 years ago. They were so close, and she was so dependent on him, and I wondered how she would ever learn to function alone. But what a privilege it has been to see the ways God has provided for my friend through the years. He has taken her step-by-step from selling a house to buying a house to selling a house to being financially comfortable enough to volunteer her time in Christian ministry. In the 16 years she has been on her own, she has learned to trust the Lord for her needs. And she has figured it out so that she has just enough money to live on while she gives away her time in the Lord's work.

And I think of others as well. Marilyn Heavilyn, who lost three sons and almost lost a grandbaby yet has touched so many through her testimony to God's goodness. Or Joni Eareckson Tada, who became a quadriplegic as a teenager but who speaks and writes and draws and sings so eloquently about God's goodness. Or Janis Willis, whose six children were killed in a highway accident but who managed to say, "I realized I had been saying, 'no, no, no,' to God as my children were entering heaven's doors. I was saying 'no, God' to the very thing I ultimately wanted most for our children—to be with God eternally.... We have thrown ourselves into God's grace."[1]

And of course my own experience reminds me again and again that God can be trusted. Again and again in my life he has given me exactly what I needed in order to grow and move toward him.

This is a God who took a little girl with good reason to distrust men and healed that distrust by giving her a husband who is strong and dependable and nurturing.

This is a God who took a willing but inexperienced young wife and put her in charge of a household of five small children (two of my own plus three of my brother's)—an effective crash course in home organization—then gave her the opportunity and the encouragement to teach others what she had learned.

This is a God who took a restless empty-nest mom and gave her a nationwide ministry of writing and speaking.

And this is a God who, again and again, has given

me the gift of his presence when I gave him the gift of my trust. When I look back at the way my life has unfolded, I can only be astonished at the wisdom and creativity of my heavenly Father.

This really is a God I can trust. In my life he has shown me again and again that he is a rock and a help and a shield, the way and the truth and the life.

And that raises another question.

Why do I still have such a hard time trusting God?

Why do I keep falling back into paralyzing fears and agonizing worries—as if God can't take care of me? Why do I keep trying to control my circumstances and my loved ones—as if God can't take care of them as well as me? Why do I keep acting as if this great trustworthy God were not capable of running the universe?

This last kind of distrust has always been a trap for me. Maybe it comes from having so much responsibility in my young life or from learning to be distrustful. But I tend to want everything to be right and good and perfect, and if things aren't running the way I think they should I tend to move in and take over. Do I want to control other people's lives when they're not moving in the direction I think they should?

No, I don't think that consciously. I just act that

way. I've done it again and again in my life—given God my trust and then taken it back and tried to run things myself.

But I am learning. I am moving forward in my ability to trust. And God is helping me do it.

You see, what I am learning is that although my trust is a gift I offer to God, I cannot offer it unless he gives it to me first. He is the source from whom all blessings flow; I cannot offer him anything he didn't originate. And yet my offering is very important.

It's like a small child buying a gift for her mother. Where does the money come from in the first place? Even if she draws her mother a picture, the crayons and the paper and even the little girl's talent came from the mother. And yet the act of giving brings such joy to both mother and child—and the child is learning valuable lessons at the same time.

So I give what I can. I offer to this great, trustworthy God my cup of fear and worry and over-control. As I hold it up to him, my cup is emptied and filled with trust and handed back to me—so I can offer it back to him.

But I don't want to get too caught up in pretty pictures here. How specifically do I hold up my cup to be filled with trust?

One way is through prayer. I need to be offering up my cup daily in the form of prayer for my family, for my church, for my children. I need to pray that they will fear the Lord and serve him. And then—this is the hardest part—I need to relinquish them, to give over those concerns to the Lord as a gesture of trust. I need to learn to pray, "God, I pray that you will do whatever it takes to transform our son or daughter or grandchild into a person who will serve you, know you, and love you with all his heart, mind, and soul. I don't know what we will have to experience before that happens. But that is my prayer."

So prayer is an offering of trust, a way to hold up my cup for filling with more trust. So is patience, being willing to wait, even when the urge to take over is strong.

I have always found it especially hard to trust God when I think something should be happening—and it isn't. Those times really tend to throw me. But I'm gradually learning to trust God even in those maddening waiting times. I've been able to look back and see that during some of those times when God didn't seem to be moving, I was moving in growth. Or I can see that if God had acted when I wanted him to, things would not have turned out so well; God's timing was far better than mine.

This brings me back again to trusting that God knows best, that he is capable of running the universe. When I wait patiently for the Lord to act in his own time, I am giving him the gift of my trust—and growing in my ability to trust.

Most of the time, though, it's not just a matter of waiting. Obedience—the willingness to follow God's nudges even when we don't completely understand why—is crucial. It's no accident that the old hymn was titled "Trust and Obey." They go together. And they're both hard. In fact, without God, they're impossible. Our cups are empty of all good things unless God is filling them.

But God does fill our cups when we hold them up. I'm learning that more and more these days. The recent unhappiness in my family has made me realize how weak my trust can be and how desperately I want to trust God. I am really seeking to trust him in every area of my life, from what happens in the next five minutes to what happens in the next five years.

And you know, the more I trust him, the more I'm learning to trust. The more I'm coming to know his character, to stare in amazement at what he's done in my life and wait in anticipation for what he's going to do next. I'm learning the truth that C.W. Christian expressed so eloquently:

> My faith is small.
> I measure it in dust
> And test its weight with straw
> And wonder that he pays me heed at all.
> How well I must
> In my self-serving supplication gall

His patience with my feeble trust.
Yet I in all fair expectation wait.
My faith is small;
My God is great.[2]

So I am learning a lot more about trust these days, and as a result, my life is much more peaceful. I also find that my perspective has sharpened; I have a clearer sense of the basic realities. I know who I can trust—and how.

I can trust God to care for me and help me grow. I can trust God to give me his presence in this life and then, when my life is over, to take me home to glory.

Most important, I can trust God to run the universe. (I don't have to.) That trust enables me to take a more lighthearted attitude toward all that concerns me.

Take my teacups, for instance.

The collection of teacups in my armoire and all around the house is one of my signatures—one of the things I'm known for. I've spoken about my teacups and written about them. They are full of memories and very precious to me, and I've always been very protective of them. But a few years ago I realized that my time was more valuable. To write or speak or minister, I needed to relinquish my house to someone who could clean for me. Relinquishing the task of cleaning the armoire with the teacups was the hardest. How could I trust anyone else with my precious collection?

Well, not long after I gave up the task, my fears were realized. The housekeeper put the shelf back in wrong; it slipped and broke some of the teacups. That was a traumatic day. But when I took my pain to God, trusting him with it, he gently and gradually changed my attitude.

I still love my teacups, but I'm not nearly as vigilant about them anymore. Now I reassure my housekeeper, "Don't be afraid of the teacups." (And I know she is more careful with them than I am.) Now I'm more likely to let little children drink tea out of my cups, to give them the gift of my trust along with the assurance that an accident won't cause me to love them any less.

For many years I have had tea parties with my granddaughter, Christine. Her brothers Chad and Bevan have enjoyed their tea parties, too. And recently when our little two-and-a-half-year-old Bradley Joe was over at the house I had a tea party with him, trusting him to drink very carefully out of one of my china teacups. I knew he could easily break that delicate cup. But I wanted to take that risk to show him how special he was to me. And he got the message. He went home and told his mother excitedly about his grownup tea party with Grammy.

Even in his baby mind, he sensed he was being trusted and he tried his best to live up to it.

And that gives me a little insight, too, into how my relationship with God works—how he fills my cup with trust.

This most trustworthy God teaches me to trust— by trusting me!

Remember, real trust is a gift you give to someone you love. It's a compliment, a gesture of respect. And it's also a way of helping them grow, to become more trustworthy.

Or put another way, when I choose to live in relationship with someone, I have to give the gift of my trust—or it's not really a relationship, just a contract.

If an employee embezzles or doesn't show up for work, it hurts the employer in the pocketbook. If that employee is also a friend, if you have a relationship, the embezzlement or absence is a betrayal of trust.

You don't have trust unless you have a relationship.

And because he wants a relationship with me, the trustworthy God who created the universe has trusted me to do his work in the world!

He has entrusted me with a family and friends and charged me with living in a way that helps them draw close to him. He has entrusted me with the job of ministry—with the women I speak to and the people who read my books and also the people I meet in the course of my everyday life. He has entrusted me with his love so that I can have a relationship with him and with others.

Do I abuse that trust?

Of course. I do it every day.

I abuse God's trust whenever I ignore one of those little nudgings of the Holy Spirit to go see someone or help someone. I abuse his trust when I snap at Bob or criticize one of my children. I abuse his trust when I fail to trust him.

But that's sort of beside the point because, in this world, if trust depended on trust never being betrayed—we'd never trust anybody. If I waited until I was sure the grandchildren would never break a teacup, I would never have a tea party with them.

Trusting is a risk you take in the interest of love. It's a calculated gamble, risking betrayal in the interest of the other person's growth. You don't necessarily trust that the other person won't do wrong, but you do trust that the person will stay in relationship with you and grow. You trust that person's basic character and potential. You trust who the person is, and who the person can be.

And that's what God does with us. The very fact that we have a life is an astounding vote of confidence on God's part. The fact that we have free will is an amazing act of trust. He's trusting that we will come to him! He's giving us room to grow.

When I was a little girl, I would sometimes wake up in the middle of the night and need to go to the bathroom. It was dark. We didn't have a night-light. So I would call out in the darkness.

"Mama, I need to go."

"Well, then, go," she would answer, her voice close and warm.

"But it's dark. I'm afraid."

Her reply came gently, assuring me of her presence, trusting me to grow.

"Be afraid," she would say, "but go."

More and more, as I grow older, I've become aware of God's love and trust working like that in my life. He allows the pain and the fear and the struggle because he trusts me to grow through them. But he's always present, a comforting, trustworthy voice in the darkness, telling me:

"Be afraid, but go. There is no place you can go that I won't be.

"Go ahead," he says. "You can trust me."

And I can.

Some Words for a Distrusting Heart

PSALM 4:8

I will both lie down in peace, and sleep; for You alone, O LORD, make me dwell in safety.

PSALM 37:1-7

Do not fret because of evildoers, nor be envious of the workers of iniquity. For they shall soon be cut down like the grass, and wither as the green herb.

Trust in the LORD, and do good; dwell in the land, and feed on His faithfulness. Delight yourself also in the LORD, and He shall give you the desires of your heart.

Commit your way to the LORD, trust also in Him, and He shall bring it to pass. He shall bring forth your righteousness as the light, and your justice as the noon-day.

Rest in the LORD, and wait patiently for Him.

PROVERBS 3:5-6

Trust in the LORD with all your heart, and lean not on your own understanding; in all your ways acknowledge Him, and He shall direct your paths.

ISAIAH 12:2

Behold, God is my salvation, I will trust and not be afraid; "For YAH, the LORD, is my strength and song; He also has become my salvation."

2 SAMUEL 22:31

As for God, His way is perfect; the word of the LORD is proven; He is a shield to all who trust in Him.

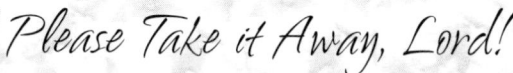

Please Take it Away, Lord!

Please take it away, Lord!
Take the anger and resentment
Out of my heavy heart.
It is not in my power to forgive
Those who have hurt me.
I need your power.
I hand over to you
The bitterness and pain,
And ask that you restore to me
A peace-filled and forgiving heart.

4

God Heals Angry Hearts

Forgive us our debts,
as we forgive our debtors.
—MATTHEW 6:12

It was an unbelievably beautiful morning in the spring. A golden sun was climbing in a brilliant blue, cloudless sky, and the sunlight sparkled in the cool air. Bob and I had decided to have our breakfast out on the patio, where the fountain was dancing with containers of pansies and mums.

Smiling at each other, we drank our orange juice and enjoyed the quiet beginning of a perfect day. Little curls of steam rose from our freshly buttered muffins as Bob read a page from a devotional for husbands and wives. We each enjoyed a cantaloupe half as we chatted about the grandchildren and the garden. Then, as we lingered over our fragrant cups of coffee, Bob pulled out our jar of Mom's Canned Questions.

A friend of ours developed this wonderful little

product, which we sell at our More Hours in My Day seminars. It's really just a decorated jar full of little slips of paper, but each slip contains a question designed to stimulate thought and discussion. We use it often when we have company and when we are by ourselves, and the questions have brought us both tears and laughter as they helped us know each other better.

As usual, Bob drew out a question and passed the jar to me. I reached in and pulled out a slip. And then I seemed to feel dark clouds rolling in to block the sunshine as I read my question. My impulse was to say "Forget it" and stuff that little slip of paper back in the jar.

What was on the paper?

Just this: "What would you do if you could spend one day with your dad?"

Such a simple question. But the memories it evoked had the power to fill my cup with pain and anger and resentment.

You see, my dad was a brilliant man, a creative Viennese chef. He used to get standing ovations for the food he prepared. From what I'm told, he doted on me as a little child, and I've inherited some of his creativity in the kitchen.

And yet my dad was also a raging alcoholic. Living in our home meant always living on edge, never knowing when he might explode. One wrong word from any of us, and the spaghetti sauce would be dumped down the toilet or down the sink; the pots and pans would be whipped off the stove and the plates off the table. There would be shouting; there would be arguments. And although my father never physically abused me, he did take his rage out on my mother and brother.

In response to my father's rage, I almost gave up talking. If saying the wrong thing could trigger an explosion, I reasoned perhaps it was better not to say anything at all. So I became intensely introverted and fearful, and I wished my father dead many times. When I was eleven, he really did die, leaving a cloud of guilt and resentment that hung over my life long after I thought I had forgotten.

Even after my dad died, I still didn't talk much. When I met Bob and we began dating, he used to say to me, "Emilie, you've got to talk." And then so many wonderful things began to happen in my life. The most important was that Bob introduced me to Jesus, and I became a Christian. Then Bob asked me to marry him, and my Jewish mama (who was very wise) surprised me by giving her consent. Relatives criticized her for letting her precious seventeen-year-old marry a Gentile, but my mama sensed that Bob could give me the love and stability I needed.

Mama was right. After Bob and I were married and I felt secure for the first time in my life, I began to talk. Now I even talk for a living—and there are probably times when Bob wishes I would stop talking!

Our lives went on. Little Jenny was born, then Brad, and I threw my energy into raising our children and making a home for us all. Bob worked as an educator, then a businessman. The kids grew up and left home. Through an amazing series of events, More Hours in My Day became a book, then an exciting ministry. My mother came to know the Messiah and moved in with us. Grandbabies were born.

Through it all, I didn't think all that much about my dad. He was in my past, which I had put behind me. I was a Christian, and I knew I was supposed to forgive others. I read in the Bible that we had to forgive if God was going to forgive us. So yes, I forgave my dad—or so I thought.

And then one day Florence Littauer invited me to go to a seminar that her friend Lana Bateman was conducting at a nearby hotel. I didn't really know what it was about, only that Florence thought it would be good for anyone. So I just walked into that hotel room...and almost immediately the tears began to flow. The spirit of God had prepared my heart for a remarkable experience in coming to terms with my past and growing closer to him. Part of what I realized that weekend was that I still had a lot of pain concerning my father. I thought I had forgiven him when I had really only boxed up my anger and resentment and stored it away—like sealing a bunch of toxic waste in a barrel and burying it underground. In order truly to forgive, I had to bring out that anger and resentment and actually hand them over to God, trusting him to take them away from me.

That weekend I began the process of truly forgiving my father and letting God restore my relationship with him. I admitted to myself that I needed healing. Even though my dad was long dead, I wrote him a long letter, pouring out both my love and my fury. I confessed the anger and bitterness I had held onto for so long without even knowing it was there.

All this was hard work. It demanded all my courage, all my energy. But what a difference that weekend made in my life. I poured out my cup of resentment. I let the Lord wash it bright and clean, and then I knew the awestruck wonder of having my cup filled to the brim with sparkling forgiveness—forgiveness for my father, and forgiveness for myself. What a wonderful feeling! I was clean, washed clean, drinking from a clean cup.

But that was not the end of the story.

Not long afterward, someone mentioned my father. And I was shocked to recognize the quick flash of anger, the stubborn, involuntary clenching of my jaw. The resentment was still there, or it had come back.

What was going on? Was that whole difficult weekend in vain?

Hadn't I emptied my cup of bitterness and let God fill it with forgiveness?

Oh yes!

The forgiveness I experienced that weekend was real. But now I was learning something very important about my cup of forgiveness.

It leaks!

For most of us, most of the time, forgiveness is an ongoing process, not a "done deal." Forgiveness is an absolute necessity for healthy living, the only known antidote to the bitterness and resentment and anger that flow naturally and abundantly when selfish human beings rub up against other selfish human beings.

But my cup of forgiveness seems to be one of the leakiest cups I own. It can be brimming over one day and empty the next—or refilled with bitter resentment over the very same hurt I thought I had forgiven. In fact, I can quickly accumulate enough pain and hurt and resentment to fill several cups, stacked up and precariously balanced.

All this can be discouraging.

"God, I thought I had let go of that!"

"God, I really want to forgive. Why is it so hard?"

But it can also be a source of faith, a reminder that we must keep going back to our forgiving Father for this cleansing elixir. We can't manufacture it ourselves; it always comes by the grace of God.

I love King David's beautiful song of forgiveness, Psalm 51. David's life was filled with one sin after another—things that were done to him and things that he did to others. But he knew the secret of coming to God for forgiveness. "Create in me a clean heart, O God," he prayed. He asked God not only to forgive, but to "wash me...whiter than snow."

How beautiful our cup can be when we offer it to the Lord—washed and cleaned, white and pure as the fresh-fallen snow, filled to the brim with beautiful, sparkling forgiveness. Why would we ever want to hold on to our scummy resentment when we could drink from that shining cup?

A friend of mine recently shared with me a great picture of how God's forgiveness works.

This friend works as a parent-aide in her daughter's third-grade class, and on one particular day she was assisting in an art lesson—a watercolor class. Each eight-year-old was given a piece of paper, a box of watercolors, a brush, a bowl of water, and a little plate for mixing colors. They were urged to experiment with colors and brush strokes, using the bowls of water to moisten the colors and to clean their brushes.

But it didn't take more than one or two dips of the brush for the water in the bowls to turn a murky gray—what the teacher called a "shadow color." And once the water was dirty, it contaminated the brighter colors. The yellows were especially vulnerable; one touch of the dark water, and the sunny yellow watercolor cake turned an ugly blackish-green.

What they needed, of course, was fresh water. So the teacher and the parent helpers began a process of moving around the room, systematically emptying the bowls and refilling the bowls with fresh water. It was a never-ending task, since the first bowls were dirty again long before the last bowls were refilled. And a few of the children didn't want their bowls refilled; they *liked* turning their paintings into muddy quagmires of brown and black. But most of the children were thrilled with the clean water, and they painted with zest, producing colorful original creations.

I've learned that forgiveness works that way, too.

I hold up my cup to be filled with sparkling clean forgiveness. And almost immediately, the resentment is creeping in—shadowy grudges from past dark memories or anger at new slights. The process of emptying out the resentment and being filled with forgiveness is an ongoing one. It has to happen again and again—as Jesus told his disciples, "seventy times seven."

Sometimes I don't want to let go of my resentment; I grow fond of my dark, murky attitudes. But when I allow an infilling of fresh "water," I am set free to live a full, creative life.

Interestingly enough, forgiveness works this way in our lives whether we're the forgivers or the "forgivees." Actually, the distinction is not all that clear, because every one of us has need to be both. Like the colors in a watercolor painting, forgiving and being forgiven run together, creating surprising and unforgettable patterns.

Every single one of us, because we are human and sinful and make mistakes and act out of motives that are less than pure, has a continual need to ask forgiveness of God and other humans.

Every single one of us, because the people around us are human and sinful and make mistakes and act out of motives that are less than pure, has constant need to forgive—or to ask God for the ability to forgive.

(We need to ask because all forgiveness—whether offered or received—is a gift of God. I can no more muster honest forgiveness on my own than my favorite teacup can fill itself with apple-cinnamon tea.)

Forgiveness, then, is an ongoing process of

filling our leaky little cups. But that isn't the whole story. Forgiveness is ongoing, but it's not an endless, repetitive cycle. Instead, forgiveness has a forward motion. It's more like a couple gracefully waltzing across the room than a dog chasing its tail.

Things change as we practice the process of forgiveness. Over time, specific hurts lose their power to hurt us (and some hurts really are healed at the moment of forgiveness). More important, emptying out anger becomes a habit. We become less likely to let hurts fester, and we become more careful of the feelings of others. More and more we grow to understand what it's like to lead a clean life. Forgiving, and being forgiven, we waltz forward along in the paths of righteousness.

My friend who helped with the art class did not have to go around emptying water bowls forever. By the time she had made several rounds, the children were learning to wipe their brushes before dipping them in the water. Beautiful pictures were emerging on the papers—a purple whale swimming in a sunset sea, a fat orange pumpkin smiling on an emerald lawn, a swirling pattern of purple and blue designs. As more paintings neared completion, there were fewer bowls to be emptied. Some of the kids who were finished even started helping with the cleanup. The class was moving along.

We never, in this life, reach a point where we don't need to forgive.

We never reach a point where we don't need forgiveness.

But we do, if we are depending on God, move closer to completion, closer to that beautiful picture he wants to paint in the world through us. We move closer to him, and we learn to follow him better.

Forgiveness is an ongoing process, but it's not an endless cycle.

I need to remember that today, because I am struggling to forgive someone I love very much. She has done some things I don't approve of, and she has hurt others whom I also love. I know that I need to forgive her, and I also need forgiveness for ways I have acted toward her. And I know this forgiveness won't come in an easy, once-and-for-all act. The hurt is too deep, the pain too immediate.

But I know forgiveness can happen, and I know the pain can heal, and I know that I can move closer and closer to forgiveness.

I know, because of what happened with my attitude toward my dad.

You see, despite the dark cloud in my soul that darkened the breakfast sunshine that morning with Bob, I really was learning to fill my cup with forgiveness. And when I read that difficult question from the jar, I felt some pain, but I did have an answer.

What would I do if I could spend a day with my dad?

First of all, I would take his hand, and we would walk and talk. "Remember, daddy?" I would say, and we would reminisce about when I was a little girl. "Remember the times you would set me up on the counter next to you while you worked? Remember when you'd take me through those big doors into the kitchens full of those great, shining pots and pans?" I always felt so proud when my daddy would introduce me to the chefs as his little girl. I always felt so safe when he held my hand.

"And, oh, daddy, I'm so sorry!" I'd tell my dad if I could spend a day with him. "I'm sorry for all the terrible things that happened to you, all the things that hurt you and made you the way you were." And I'd say, "Daddy, I know why you drank. I know why you were full of fury. You had so much pain in your heart, in your cup—from being abandoned when your parents died and being raised in the kitchen in the palace of Vienna. And you have so much pain from being a Jew in Nazi-occupied Austria, and having to change your name to escape, and fighting in the war and being shot three times."

Daddy used to show us the scars from those gun-shot wounds, but it was the deeper, hidden scars that caused him more pain. In so many ways his life was nothing but a battle. No wonder he tried to blot it out with alcohol.

If I could spend a day with my dad, I wouldn't want to deny the pain that he caused me. It was real, and I've learned that denying real pain hinders forgiveness instead of helping it. But I would also want to tell my dad that I love him. I would want to thank him for what he gave me—my creativity, my talent with food, the love he poured on me when he wasn't drinking.

And more than anything else, I would want to tell my dad that we have a heavenly Father who can cover the hurt and pain and take it from us. I would want him to know, more than anything else, my dearest friend, the Messiah, the Lord Jesus, the One who said, "Forgive, and you will be forgiven" (Luke 6:37).

I can't do that, of course. I can't spend another day with my dad, and that will always be a source of sadness for me. But I know I have finally come to a place in my life where memories of him are no longer a source of bitterness for me. Forgiveness has finally cleansed the area of my heart where those memories reside. And because that is true, I am more confident that other areas can be cleansed as well. Because I know forgiveness works, I am more ready to waltz another round.

Forgiveness works, even when you can't tell it's working. Even when you don't feel forgiven or don't feel forgiving. Even when you don't particularly want to forgive, when you find yourself grumping to God, "All right, I'll forgive since you say so, but…"

And forgiveness works no matter what the forgiveness issues are in your life.

Perhaps your spouse has been unfaithful or your son has adopted a lifestyle you cannot approve. Perhaps a friend has said something cruel behind your back or a colleague has attacked you publicly. Perhaps you are struggling with ongoing bitterness over something that happened years ago.

Or perhaps you need forgiveness for yourself. Perhaps you are overwhelmed with guilt or simply miserable because a relationship has been ruptured. Perhaps you are furious with yourself over a thoughtless remark, or you are beginning to be convicted of a hidden sin that is keeping you from fellowship with God.

Whatever in your life is causing you pain, you don't need to let resentment fill your cup. Above all, you don't need to hold on to the bitter brew.

Forgiveness works. You can take your cup to the Lord and ask him to empty it of resentment and guilt, to fill it with sparkling forgiveness. In Christ you can find the strength, if it's appropriate, to go to the other people involved and ask for forgiveness—and you can find the grace to accept forgiveness from God if the other person is not ready to grant it. Even if the other people involved are no longer in your life—or no longer living—you can write them a letter and pour out your heart. Do whatever it takes to remove the cloud and cleanse your soul and set you again on the paths of rightness.

Be prepared to do it again, if necessary—even seventy times seven times. But remember that if you've asked, God has answered. First John 1:9 assures us, "If we confess our sins, He is faithful and just to forgive us our sins and to cleanse us from all unrighteousness."

This is so vital to remember in those times when, for one reason or another, the forgiveness doesn't seem to be working.

I know of a woman who went through a bad time in her marriage and made a series of painful mistakes. She fell apart emotionally, the marriage split up, and her husband was granted custody of their two young children. Although she wrote them faithfully, they were very angry and wanted nothing to do with her. Unfortunately, her ex-husband was very bitter and inflamed these feelings of anger. Eventually he moved them to a state so distant that she could barely afford to visit (although she tried).

During all this time, the woman worked very hard to rebuild her life. She relied on a competent counselor and support groups. She also returned to the faith she had left behind many years earlier. On her knees she expressed her repentance to God and begged forgiveness for her part in all that had happened. She also wrote her children and asked their forgiveness for anything she had done to hurt them.

After that, the problems continued. Her ex-husband was still hostile, and he even used her requests for forgiveness to try to deny her visitation. Her children were still distant. They were so far away that visits were a severe financial hardship. She struggled with guilt for what she had done and deep worry about her children's future.

So she went to her pastor with her pain.

"I've asked God to forgive me," she said. "And I really think he has. So why don't I feel forgiven? And why is everything still so hard?"

That wise pastor looked at her with great compassion. "If you've asked the Lord for forgiveness, he *has* forgiven you. So maybe what you need now is not forgiveness, but the grace to live with the consequences of your actions."

That has been a very helpful word for me during the times in my life when forgiveness just doesn't seem to work.

Forgiveness is not a superglue for broken relationships. It's not an eraser for hurtful remarks or painful memories. And forgiveness doesn't excuse us from having to cope with the consequences of sin in our lives and the lives of others.

Forgiveness works, but it works at the soul level, sometimes deeper than we can see. And that is why forgiveness doesn't seem to change anything—at least not right away.

True forgiveness—given or received—works because it changes me.

But that, of course, changes everything.

Some Words for an Angry Heart

MATTHEW 18:21-22

Then Peter came to Him and said, "Lord, how often shall my brother sin against me, and I forgive him? Up to seven times?"

Jesus said to him, "I do not say to you, up to seven times, but up to seventy times seven."

PSALM 37:8-9

Cease from anger, and forsake wrath; do not fret—it only causes harm. For evildoers shall be cut off; but those who wait on the LORD, they shall inherit the earth.

MATTHEW 6:14-15

For if you forgive men their trespasses, your heavenly Father will also forgive you. But if you do not forgive men their trespasses, neither will your Father forgive your trespasses.

LUKE 17:3-4

Take heed to yourselves. If your brother sins against you, rebuke him; and if he repents, forgive him. And if he sins against you seven times in a day, and seven times in a day returns to you, saying, "I repent," you shall forgive him.

EPHESIANS 4:31-32

Let all bitterness, wrath, anger, clamor, and evil speaking be put away from you, with all malice. And be kind to one another, tenderhearted, forgiving one another, even as God in Christ forgave you.

You Have Overcome the World!

You have overcome the world, Lord!
And that means you have overcome
All the trouble in it as well!
You strengthen
And establish
And restore support to me
When I feel overwhelmed with trouble.
You walk with me
Through the dark shadows of life
And you bless me
With your gifts of goodness and mercy.

5

God Heals Troubled Hearts

I have told you these things, so that in me you may have peace. In this world you will have trouble. But take heart! I have overcome the world.

—JOHN 16:33

I never thought it would happen to me.

But then, most of us never do.

Yes, we know there will be times of pain and difficulty and sadness. The Bible is quite blunt about it: "In this world," said Jesus, "you will have trouble." Years later, the apostle Peter wrote that we shouldn't be surprised by suffering or think it an abnormal thing.

But still, we *are* surprised when bad things happen to us.

At some level, I guess, we all believe we will be an exception, that the pain and suffering that infect the world will somehow bypass us. Or if we've already endured times of pain, we assume we've somehow been inoculated to avoid further trauma.

But life simply doesn't work that way.

Have you found that out, too?

In this world, difficulty is part of the general forecast. Sometimes the trouble comes in torrents. And although we have been told to expect it, as often as not it seems to hit from an unexpected angle.

That's how it felt to me. I should have known better. But I never saw it coming.

Just so you'll know the background, I want to tell you the outlines of my story. But even as I tell it, I'm aware that your story may top mine. You may have known far more pain and fear and worry in your circumstances, or you may know someone whose pain and fear and worry make mine look almost petty. *I* know people like this—people whose stories leave me humbled and amazed.

But I'm not writing to swap war stories. I am writing to testify to what I have learned from a God who promises to bring us through floods undrowned, through fires unburned. Besides, I have learned over the years that each person's trouble is unique to him or her, but that in sharing our stories we can often find common ground. So let me tell you just a little about the years when my cup overflowed with trouble, hoping that, somehow, the telling will help you in your own pain and encourage you to tell your own story.

For me, the "dark years" all started four years ago when our daughter, our precious Jenny, took her three young children and left her husband.

I was devastated. I never thought something like that could happen in our family.

Yes, I knew all about the divorce rate in our society. I was well aware that even Christian homes are not immune. But now my own family, so precious to my heart, so lovingly nurtured over the years, was being ripped apart. And when that happened, something deep inside of me ruptured as well.

On the one hand, I knew that my daughter had been deeply unhappy. And yet I believed so strongly in the sanctity of marriage. I was convinced that, with work and attention, even a difficult marriage could survive. (I still believe these things, with all my heart.) I hurt for my son-in-law, who seemed devastated by my daughter's departure. My heart bled for those three children, my grandchildren, who loved their mother and daddy and wanted only for their home to be whole again. And I was full of fear and worry for my Jenny, who seemed so angry and rebellious and far from being the kind of mother those children needed.

You see, when our Jenny left her husband, she left her God as well.

And I, who spoke about happy homes to hundreds of women a week, was helpless to do anything about the breakup of this home and the pain of these people I loved so very deeply.

Even now, it's hard for me to express the depth of the anguish I felt over this circumstance. I wanted with every fiber of my body for that broken home to be healed, for the pain to be erased from my grandchildren's faces, for my daughter and son-in-law to find each other again.

And it just wasn't happening.

Weeks passed, then months, then years, and the reality of that broken home didn't change— although, as I would see later, God was working to redeem the situation in surprising ways. Meanwhile, either coincidentally or because of the stress, I began to get sick.

It began with chronic bouts of bronchitis, one of those irritating illnesses where you cough and cough and don't seem to get better. Series after series of antibiotics didn't seem to help. Neither did sinus surgery. Referred to an allergist, I was soon taking three allergy shots a week.

And that was only the beginning. The bronchitis persisted, along with other strange symptoms, such as mosquito bites that itched fiercely and refused to heal. I had gained a little weight, and though I "cleaned up" pretty well for seminars, I was beginning to think that something was seriously wrong with me.

Through this all, though, I continued with my busy schedule of giving More Hours in My Day seminars. I wrote books. I even began, tentatively, to share my pain about Jenny in both the seminars and the books. Women were responding. My ministry was growing.

And all the while, I was doing everything I knew to get better. You see, I'm the kind of person who has always been teased for my healthy lifestyle. I take vitamins. I eat right and exercise regularly. I've even coauthored a book on healthy eating! Now, faced with illness, I redoubled my efforts. I watched my diet carefully and took a lot of vitamins, applying everything I knew about good nutrition. I showed up faithfully for my allergy shots. I took full advantage of our summer and winter rest periods and tried to get enough sleep. I carefully researched the many books and tapes sent to me by concerned friends, and I followed the suggestions of the ones that seemed sound.

Finally, when nothing seemed to help, I dug out a name that I had jotted down at a conference years before. A sweet woman in Arkansas had shared the name of a nutritional consultant in our area, a Christian woman with a Ph.D. in nutrition and a specialization in homeopathic remedies. I called this

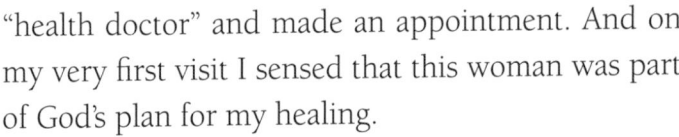

"health doctor" and made an appointment. And on my very first visit I sensed that this woman was part of God's plan for my healing.

We talked at length about what had been happening to me, what I had been doing to help myself, and what treatments my doctors had prescribed. And I shared with this health doctor something that I had begun to notice—that I actually felt better in the weeks when I missed my allergy shots. Working together, she and I finally determined that the combination of antibiotics and allergy shots and perhaps other factors I didn't know of had combined to poison my system. I was experiencing toxic overload. My immune system was at zero, and my body had reached the point where it could not even assimilate the vitamins and minerals I was putting into it.

Now, I want to make something very clear at this point. I am *not* saying that traditional allergy treatments are harmful or that homeopathic treatment is better than traditional medicine. I am not even saying that my medical doctors were wrong and my health doctor was right. Every body is different, and I believe God heals each of us in different ways: through traditional medicine, through alternative medicine, even through spontaneous healing. As I visited this nutritional consultant, however, I felt a strong confirmation in my spirit that the path she pointed to was the right path for me to take. So I made the decision to quit my allergy-shot regimen, and with the nutritionist's help I began a program of detoxifying my body through diet.

I thought it was working, though the process itself was not pleasant. The very process of ridding one's body of toxins can involve quite a bit of discomfort: nausea, excessive perspiration, and other unpleasant sensations. But I thought I could feel my healthy, carefully chosen diet working. I began losing some weight—again, I was sure, because of the diet. And in some ways I could feel myself growing stronger. For a few months I was even free of the bronchitis. But then it returned with a vengeance, along with chills, vomiting, and fever.

Somehow, through it all, God was still giving me the strength I needed to do what he had called me to do: to get up on that platform and speak, and to talk and minister to women afterward. So many times I would stand by that platform wondering if I would even be able to climb the steps. And then God would take over and do his work, and I would speak and my heart would swell to see the work God was doing in the lives of the women at that seminar. Even in my depleted state, I rejoiced in what God was doing. But I also knew something was deeply wrong with my body, and I still didn't know what it was.

My weight loss continued and accelerated. People began to comment on how thin I looked. I suffered with night sweats and nausea, and I still couldn't stop coughing.

Then finally my family put their foot down.

My daughter Jenny made me an appointment to see a doctor, who took some tests and then referred me to a Christian oncologist. And after a round of blood tests and other diagnostics we had a name for the illness that was behind so many of my symptoms:

chronic lymphatic leukemia.

Cancer.

The very name was terrifying. And now the doctors were talking about further tests and treatments involving radiation and chemotherapy. They explained that though this particular form of leukemia moves relatively slowly and that I could live with it a long time, it was still very serious and needed to be treated right away. I needed some tests involving radiation, and then I needed to start a program of chemotherapy.

After my previous experience, my very soul shrank from the thought of these procedures, which involved injecting more chemicals into my body. So I went to my health doctor for advice. I sat there in her office, weeping and shaking and painfully thin, and I told her what the diagnosis had been.

What she said was, "Give me two weeks." She asked me to wait at least that long before I agreed to any more tests or treatment. "If you let them subject your body to all that," she said, "you risk undoing everything we've worked so hard to do. So at least give me two weeks to prepare you and build you up for treatment."

Now I was heartsick, pulled between the advice of my health doctor, whom I respected so deeply; my oncologist, whom I had also grown to trust; my family, who loved me and wanted me to be well; and my own desire not to fill my body full of chemicals again. So I prayed, and I talked to friends, and I prayed some more, and I finally told my Bob I wanted to give my health doctor the two weeks she requested. I expected him to resist, but to my surprise he agreed.

It turned out to be more than two weeks. The combination of holidays and commitments kept me away from that doctor's office until six weeks later. Meanwhile, I had begun a special diet and a course of homeopathic treatment to build up my body. I had been asking for prayer from everyone I knew. My health doctor and my oncologist were praying for me. My friends were praying for me. Women I met at conferences were praying for me, and I received cards and letters from people I didn't even know who had learned what I was going through and promised me their prayers. I knew I was being surrounded by a powerful prayer shield.

And then I went back to my Christian oncologist, bracing myself for the tests and treatments I feared.

Before he started, though, he tested my blood again. And with a look of surprise on his face he asked me, "What have you been doing? This is very impressive."

Then he told me that my white blood cell count, which had been very high six weeks earlier, was now almost normal, and well out of the danger range. My other indicators had subsided as well.

"It was prayer," I told him with wonder. "Prayer and homeopathic treatments."

That good Christian man just looked at me. "I believe in prayer," he said, "and I have no problem with alternative treatments. I suggest you just keep doing what you're doing." He also said, "I see no reason to proceed with the tests and the chemotherapy at this time."

Hallelujah! What a victory. We left that office praising God almost hysterically. Vastly relieved, I rejoiced that God was healing me, and I dedicated myself to rest and building up my strength for yet another busy fall season. Step by step, day by day, I could feel myself growing stronger, praising God, eager to get back to work...until that day a little more than two months later when I went to change the sheets on our bed and ended up doubled over in agony.

I had never felt such a pain as this searing and stabbing deep in my abdomen. I could barely make it to the couch to lie down. By the time Bob and Jenny loaded me into our van and headed for the hospital, I was curled into a fetal position, holding my stomach and moaning.

That night, I underwent emergency surgery for a perforated ulcer the size of a silver dollar.

I was in the hospital for more than a week. We had to cancel seven seminars, something I had not done during my whole long siege with bronchitis, chemical poisoning, or even leukemia. Bob was stressed with handling the details of our business and trying to take care of me. I had a book deadline staring me in the face. And Jenny's family was still not together!

My health doctor assured me (when I could speak again) that this was not a setback. But it felt like one, and just when I was finally getting better. Would life ever feel good again?

That was four months later. And that, so far, is the story of my "rainy years," when my cup has overflowed with pain and fear and uncertainty and worry and weakness…but also with the miracles of God working in and through my life.

And the story still goes on. My stitches have healed, my bland ulcer diet gave way to my nutritionist's strength diet, I resumed my conference schedule. Jenny and her husband had not reconciled, but God was working other amazing miracles in my daughter's life in the meantime.

So things were better.

But in just a few weeks I was terrified to feel another pain in my stomach, almost a reprise of that awful, searing ulcer pain.

It was not serious this time, just an excess of stomach acid.

But it was a sobering experience—a reminder that, ultimately, I am not in control of any of the things life pours into my cup. My troubles might well continue. I may never get well. My family may never be put back together the way it was before.

It could be one thing after another for the rest of my life. There is nothing I can do to keep my cup from overflowing with trouble.

Except for one thing.

There is one thing that I, and you, and anyone who is facing trouble can do and must do, again and again.

We can carry that overflowing cup, messy and sloppy as it is, to the foot of the cross and leave it there.

Through prayer, through holy imagination, through an act of the will, we can surrender that cup of pain to the Lord, so that he can deal with the overflow of trouble.

You see, the only antidote that I know for a cup overflowing with trouble is a cup overflowing with the love of Christ.

And he gives us that.

I knew it before I went through these years of agony, but now I know it in a far deeper part of my soul. I have felt his touch, his provision, at a cell level, deep in my being. I have witnessed his healing, redemptive power at work in my life even when things seemed darkest.

I have seen his work in the lives of others, as well, and that brings me hope and encouragement.

Not long ago, for example, I received a wonderful letter from a woman named Barbara who had grown up in a sexually abusive home. She cannot remember a time in her childhood when she was not abused. Barbara married and had a child but was widowed suddenly at age twenty-five. When she remarried, her first husband's parents disowned both her and her child.

Talk about years of trouble! But somehow, through all that, this woman was able to remain open to God's healing, or, as she puts it, "Jesus loved me through it all." She remarried and raised a family. Now, at age fifty-four, she is finishing graduate school with a degree in counseling and preparing to embark on a new career and a new ministry. She writes, "At this point in my life, God has a real call on my life. I haven't a clue where he is taking me, but I am enjoying the trip."

Or I think of a dear man we know, our former pastor, who has gone through one tragedy after another: the loss of his home to fire (twice!), the loss of a wife, who became an alcoholic and eventually committed suicide, and the loss of a son, who was paralyzed in an auto accident and died at an early age. Whenever I think of this man, who has endured so much, I am amazed by his gentle, compassionate spirit, his commitment to ministry, the underlying joy in his heart that could come only from having his cup filled by the Holy Spirit.

Again and again I have seen this happen—God working in the lives of men and women who bring their overflowing cups of suffering to him and allow him to refill their cups with his love. And again and again, even in the midst of my own suffering, I have seen him do it for me as well.

It hasn't always come the way I expected. One thing I have learned from this rainy season in my life is that God gives us what we need, not always what we want. He gives us what we need to grow and draw closer to him and accomplish his purposes, and my own peace and joy depend in part on accepting what he chooses to give me.

But that doesn't mean I have to *like* what life hands out to me!

I can't find any recommendation in God's Word that I'm supposed to be glad that my daughter's marriage is unhappy, that my grandchildren are torn in half, or that my body is sick and the doctors can't figure out what is wrong. I don't have to like the pain that sears my abdomen or the cancer that saps my strength.

I can pray to avoid suffering and even pray for it to be taken away. Jesus himself asked to be spared the cup of his own suffering and death.

And I'm not even required to refrain from complaining when my cup is full of suffering. Like Job or David, I can cry out to God and tell him exactly how I feel; I can even tell him I don't feel he's doing things right. The Psalms are absolutely filled with people fussing and fuming at God because life is not happening to them the way they would like it to happen. (One day, when I was feeling especially unhappy, I opened the book of Psalms and read page after page of "complaining" out loud to God!)

And somewhere along the line, of course, I inevitably found myself asking the *why* questions: Why me? Why now? Why me and not someone else?

I've asked those questions plenty of times, sometimes angrily, sometimes plaintively, sometimes with a sense of embarrassment.

Why embarrassment?

Because I really know the answer, of course.

Or at least I know the real question:

Why *not* me?

In this world, Jesus assures us, we *will* have trouble. He of all people knew what it was to suffer undeservedly. In all the pain I have suffered over the years, I have had but a tiny taste of what he went through on my account.

And yet, in the very next breath, Jesus reminds me that no matter what our pain, we still have a reason to hope.

"In this world you will have trouble," he said. "But take heart! I have overcome the world."

We shouldn't be surprised, Peter reminds us, when we have pain in our lives. That's the inevitable result of living here on this fallen planet in vulnerable bodies, with weak spirits and fallible souls. But Peter, near the end of his epistle, adds a ringing promise that picks up shine and polish and meaning for me each time I read it again. It's one of the verses that kept me hoping and moving forward when I felt like I couldn't go on.

"After you have suffered for a little while," the apostle writes, "the God of all grace, who has called you to his eternal glory in Christ, will himself restore, support, strengthen, and establish you."

It's a given, in other words, that from time to

time, or even most of the time, our cups will overflow with trouble.

But our eternal God, in his eternal mercy, will use that trouble to restore and support and strengthen and establish us. Even as we walk through the dark shadows, even in the presence of our enemies, our cup will overflow with his goodness and mercy.

I believe it.

I have seen it, even in the midst of the worst seven years of my life. I have seen it in my own circumstances and in the lives of so many whose faith and courage and trust inspire me.

And now, when the clouds seem to be lifting and the colors begin to shine through the clouds (but who knows what will happen in the future?), I can see so much more clearly the ways in which I have indeed been restored, supported, strengthened, and established. It didn't happen exactly the way I thought it would, but the results were so much deeper and more wonderful than I could imagine.

I really never thought it all would happen to me.

Neither did you.

But you and I could never know the wonderful things that God has in store for us when we bring him our overflowing cup of trouble, let him empty the pain, and then let him fill us to overflowing with his love.

Some Words for a Troubled Heart

Psalm 23:4-6

Yea, though I walk through the valley of the shadow of death, I will fear no evil; for You are with me; Your rod and Your staff, they comfort me.

You prepare a table before me in the presence of my enemies; You anoint my head with oil; my cup runs over.

Surely goodness and mercy shall follow me all the days of my life; and I will dwell in the house of the Lord forever.

James 1:2-4

My brethren, count it all joy when you fall into various trials, knowing that the testing of your faith produces patience. But let patience have its perfect work, that you may be perfect and complete, lacking nothing.

Psalm 9:9

The Lord also will be a refuge for the oppressed, a refuge in times of trouble.

God Heals Troubled Hearts

1 Peter 4:12-13

Beloved, do not think it strange concerning the fiery trial which is to try you, as though some strange thing happened to you; but rejoice to the extent that you partake of Christ's sufferings, that when His glory is revealed, you may also be glad with exceeding joy.

Psalm 138:7

Though I walk in the midst of trouble, You will revive me; You will stretch out Your hand against the wrath of my enemies, and Your right hand will save me.

Nahum 1:7

The Lord is good, a stronghold in the day of trouble; and He knows those who trust in Him.

Romans 5:1-4

Therefore, having been justified by faith, we have peace with God through our Lord Jesus Christ, through whom also we have access by faith into this grace in which we stand, and rejoice in hope of the glory of God.

And not only that, but we also glory in tribulations, knowing that tribulation produces perseverance; and perseverance, character; and character, hope.

2 CORINTHIANS 1:3-4

Blessed be the God and Father of our Lord Jesus Christ, the Father of mercies and God of all comfort, who comforts us in all our tribulation, that we may be able to comfort those who are in any trouble, with the comfort with which we ourselves are comforted by God.

I Need Help, Lord!

I need help, Lord.
I don't like to admit that, but it's true.
I'm so used to taking care of myself,
I'm not even sure how to be helped.
I've never really learned to lean on anyone.
Help me learn to accept the help you give me,
From the people you graciously place in my life
As well as directly from you.

6

God Heals Lonely Hearts

For where two or three are gathered together
in My name, I am there in the midst of them.
—Matthew 18:20

It's one of my favorite times of day.

The sun has set. The phone has stopped ringing. (I hope!) The conference schedules are filed away, and the dishwasher is finishing up the last of the mealtime chores. A little fire in the fireplace chases away the chill, while a string quartet plays merrily on the CD.

Bob is comfortable in his big green leather easy chair, an afghan on his lap and a book in his hand. Every few minutes he stops to read me a passage while I putter in the kitchen, preparing our evening cup of tea.

I don't hurry as I pour the boiling water into the teapot. The delightful scent of cinnamon starts to waft around the kitchen as I gather together lace napkins, china cups, sugar, and cream. A candle in a crystal holder casts a golden glow, a single daisy plucked from an arrangement in the hall smiles from a miniature vase. I rummage quietly in the pantry to find a few cookies, and I know there's a bunch of grapes in the refrigerator.

The tea is steeped. I carry the tray into our peaceful living room.

Bob moves his feet from the hassock to make room for the tray. I curl up on the carpet beside him and pour. And then while the fire crackles and the music dances, we talk quietly or we pray or we just sit and share our cup of cinnamon tea and sharing—our delicious cup of communion.

Communion, you see, is not just another name for the Lord's Supper—although the ritual of bread and wine embodies that reality on the most profound level.

Communion is also the appropriate word for what happens whenever spirits are shared and cups are filled with love and mutual participation. It's what happens whenever human beings draw near to each other and to God, managing somehow to emerge from their separateness and partake of the shared life God intended.

You see, God never intended for us to be alone. He said that from the beginning. He made us for each other and for fellowship with him.

Our separateness, our deep-seated loneliness,

that familiar sense of being all alone in a body with "me, me, me"—that's our own doing. It's the long-term result of that long-ago choice to listen to a serpent, eat an apple, take charge of our own destiny. Because we are sinful, there's a part of us that always wants to hide from God and each other.

And then we feel so alone, even in the midst of a crowd. Even in the bustle of our work, the warmth of our families. By ourselves we are just ourselves, and our cups are full of ourselves only.

That's why those moments of true communion are so delicious. They are a pure gift, a generous outpouring from the God whose very nature is relationship. (For what is the holy Trinity but an intertwined relationship of three identities—Father, Son, and Holy Spirit?) It is my loving Lord who empties my cup of loneliness and selfishness and pours for me my cup of communion.

That doesn't mean that people who don't know God cannot enjoy moments of special sharing or even deep connection. It doesn't mean you have to be a Christian in order to enjoy closeness and friendship. In a sense, the cup of communion is a gift from creation, part of how we are made. God created us to connect to each other, and even our sinful separation has not negated that built-in capacity. God made us with the need for other people and the desire to live in harmony instead of discord, sharing instead of separation, fulfillment instead of loneliness. He created us with the physical and emotional tools we need to connect with each other—eyes, hands, voices, sympathy, loyalty, understanding. Human beings do manage to make some connections with each other while living apart from God.

And yet there is something so different, something so special about the cup of communion that is poured for me when I bring my cup of loneliness to the throne of God and hold it up to be washed and refilled with sharing and closeness and love. It's like the difference between muddy pond water and water from a flowing spring. It sparkles.

That's why, although I may have good and even loving relationships with men and women who don't know Christ—and there are many in my family— the relationships I share with my Christian brothers and sisters are different. It's more than just having a belief or a cause in common. It's having a *life* in common. When even two or three of us are gathered in the Lord's name, the presence of the Holy Spirit adds a sparkling eternal dimension to our human communion.

I cannot even begin to imagine what our marriage would be like without that eternal dimension. My Bob, who is very wise, knew from the beginning that we would have little chance of going the distance without having a closeness in that area. Even though he was attracted to me and respected my Jewish heritage, he held back. Instead of courting me, he shared his faith with me. And only when we had come to share a commitment to Jesus Christ as the Messiah did he propose marriage.

Over and over in my life I have thanked the Lord for Bob's strength and wisdom, for we have needed the spiritual communion of our shared faith to get through the tough times in our life together. My husband has always been my best friend, and being able to pray together and read Scripture together and talk together about the Lord and work together in ministry has been a privilege and a joy. In my marriage, God has poured out his cup of communion with overflowing generosity.

And there are other ways God fills my cup with communion. I have always loved sharing my faith with our children and especially with the grandchildren. I love to see them growing in the Lord, even through their painful experiences. In many ways they minister to me, and I rejoice to see that they have a spiritual foundation I never had at their age.

My church family, too, offers me so many opportunities to come out of my loneliness and share a cup of communion. Bob and I have developed deep and meaningful friendships in this body. I love the sense of spiritual sharing I feel when we sing and study and serve together, and especially when we gather together at the Lord's table to remember his ultimate act of sharing.

Even closer to my heart than my church family is my special adopted family of prayer partners. These are my close-to-the-heart friends whose love has stood the test of time. These are the people I call when my heart is aching, the ones I trust above all others to pray with me. They are all so different—Yoli and Barbara and Donna. But they are truly the sisters of my heart. They are the ones I trust not only with my tears, but with my puffy red eyes and unsightly runny nose and scrunched-up crying face. They have truly been God's gift of communion to me.

But my cup of communion is not just filled among the people I know. My kinship with other brothers and sisters in Christ has brought Bob and me into "family reunions" across the nation. This is one of the most amazing surprises God has given me over my lifetime (and there have been so many surprises!). He has used our ministry of teaching and writing not only to do his work of touching lives and reclaiming spirits, but also to fill our cups with sparkling Christian communion.

We are on the road nearly every week, traveling to lead seminars in towns we've never visited before. We've reached the point where we can almost predict what will happen. Someone we have never seen will meet us at the airport. For three or four days we will pray together and eat together and work together and perhaps live together with people with whom we may have little in common but a shared desire to serve the Lord. And then, by the time the weekend is over, our cup of communion will be filled. We are all fast friends. Sometimes we will end up being in touch for years.

It doesn't just happen with seminars, either. By God's grace, I have been able to share deeply with people I will never meet, women I encounter only as a voice on the phone or a face at a conference or a folded-up sheet of notepaper in an envelope. Somehow God uses what I say or do to touch these women. Somehow they find the courage to come to me with their pain. And somehow, as we talk together or pray together, he fills both our cups with a special kind of communion.

But perhaps you are a bit fed up by now with my litany of communion. Perhaps you are going through a lonely time. Perhaps you are grieving the loss of someone you loved or having difficulty making friends. Perhaps you feel isolated and alone in the midst of your family or your church, and my stories about a close marriage or a loving church family or sympathetic friends just leave you feeling hollow.

I understand if you feel that way.

You see, the very reason my cups of communion

seem so amazing is that my cup was very full of loneliness for most of my life. I am an introverted person by nature, and the pain of living in an alcoholic home wrapped me further in a shell of separateness. I grew up feeling different and alone, and I would never have considered bringing other children home to my disordered household. Then, after my father died, I was too busy trying to keep house for my mother and manage my schoolwork to have time for friends—even if I could come out of myself enough to make one.

And even though God in his amazing mercy has granted me the gift of a good marriage and good friendships, I don't always feel like my cup of communion is filled. There are many times when I struggle with a private grief in the midst of a public crowd. Sometimes I can be in church or with Bob and feel like I'm a million miles away. And I still find that my best friends are those who reach out to me first, those who don't wait for me to reach out to them.

My cup of communion—like so many of my "earthen vessel" cups—is a leaky one, and when the sharing drains away I often find I'm the same shy little girl who hid behind her mother's skirts.

I know I'm not the only one who feels this way. All of our cups are leaky when it comes to communion. Even though we were created for sharing, we are also flawed by sin, and sin is separation—from God and from other human beings. We are made for relationships, but we are also selfish, and we suffer from the selfishness of others. We yearn to be close to others, but we are also lonely to the core, still locked inside our own skulls, unable on our own to truly understand or reach out.

So even though we were created for communion, communion is still a miracle.

Without the miracle of communion, friendships go flat, church friends betray each other, marriages dissolve into separateness or fall apart altogether. Without the miracle of communion I am left with only me. But with the miracle of communion I am filled.

And here's the biggest miracle of all. I don't have to make friends or influence people in order to have my cup filled with communion. I don't even need to be with other people.

Sometimes my heavenly Father does fill my cup of communion through my relationships with Bob or my children or my church or my prayer partners or the people who come to my seminars.

But always—with or without other people—he fills my cup of communion with himself. My most satisfying cup of sharing comes in my relationship with him.

Over the years, I have learned that Jesus is the

One I can always trust, the One I can always talk to, the One whose love truly changes my life.

I know that I can talk to the Lord and say, "Today I'm not feeling that I can trust. Today I'm not sure that I like my Bob too much. Today I'm really upset with the children." The one thing I really have experienced with the Lord is that I can tell him anything, that he's not going to tell anybody else, and that he's going to comfort me and forgive and love me.

That's what a real friend is, isn't it?

A friend can love you in spite of who you are.

A friend can comfort you wherever you are.

A friend can speak to you in honesty but then encourage you to move on to the next step.

A friend can fill your cup with sharing and closeness and love—with communion.

The old hymn really had it right: "What a Friend We Have in Jesus."

The older I get, the more I long for that friendship with my Lord to grow. I realize there isn't anything else on this earth that can give me more joy or fulfillment or strength. I want to talk with him, to share my life with him, to hold my cup of communion up to be filled with him. I want my Lord to use me, to live in me, to fill others' cups through me.

No, I don't always get it right. I don't always feel close to Jesus—anymore than I always feel close to Bob or our children or our fellow creatures. As long as I live in this sin-touched body and in this sin-touched world, my cup will leak.

That is why I must constantly pray—

Lord, I'm lonely. Fill my cup.

Lord, I've been so caught up in myself I can't even think about Bob or Jenny or Yoli or anybody else. Fill my cup.

Lord, I've been trying to do it all by myself again. I've been trying to go it on my own. And I don't want to do it anymore.

Fill my cup, Lord, with communion.

Fill my cup, Lord, with you.

Some Words for a Lonely Heart

PSALM 133:1
Behold, how good and how pleasant it is
for brethren to dwell together in unity!

GENESIS 2:18
It is not good that man should be alone.

PSALM 68:6

God sets the solitary in families; He brings out those who are bound into prosperity.

1 JOHN 1:7

But if we walk in the light as He is in the light, we have fellowship with one another, and the blood of Jesus Christ His Son cleanses us from all sin.

PHILIPPIANS 1:3

I thank my God upon every remembrance of you.

ECCLESIASTES 4:9-12

Two are better than one, because they have a good reward for their labor. For if they fall, one will lift up his companion. But woe to him who is alone when he falls, for he has no one to help him up. Again, if two lie down together, they will keep warm; but how can one be warm alone? Though one may be overpowered by another, two can withstand him. And a threefold cord is not quickly broken.

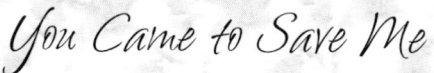

You Came to Save Me

Thank you, Jesus,
For coming into this world to save me,
And not to condemn me.
It can be hard to hold my head up
When the world insists on beating down on me.
I thank you
For your unconditional acceptance of me.
Help me remember
To in turn not criticize those around me,
But to build others up
With encouragement.

7

God Heals Discouraged Hearts

For God did not send His son into the world to condemn the world, but that the world through Him might be saved.
—JOHN 3:17

"What a beautiful reception," I thought as I flipped through the recently developed stack of photographs.

There was my newly married niece, her face flushed with happiness. There was her new husband, beaming and proud. There were the children, dressed up and excited, and the older ladies beaming with satisfaction at another wedding in the family.

And there I was in my white Battenburg lace dress—looking pretty good, if I did say so myself!

I should have looked good. I had poured a lot of effort into pulling myself together perfectly for the occasion, paying special attention to my hair, my hose, my shoes, my bag. Trying so hard to get everything just exactly right so that my elderly auntie, for once, would have nothing to criticize.

Well, I finally did it, I thought as I flipped another picture. There was my aunt sitting at her table with a big smile on her face. My smile was big, too, as I remembered it. For the first time in my memory, she hadn't said a single critical word about how I was dressed or how my makeup looked or anything else. I'd talked to her on the phone several times since then, and she still hadn't made a negative comment.

I glanced at the clock. I really needed to call her again. She was very independent, even in her eighties, but I still tried to check on her every day or two.

Auntie was in a wonderful mood when she answered the phone. She had gotten her pictures, too. So we reminisced about the ceremony, speculated on how the new couple would get along, and replayed the events of the reception.

"And, oh, Emilie," she enthused, "you looked just beautiful."

By now I was actually grinning. This was almost too good to be true.

And then she added in a thoughtful voice, "Emilie...you really need to consider getting a padded bra."

Zing. I could feel my grin slipping down to the floor, that old familiar knot tightening my stomach.

I should have seen it coming, of course. It was only the hundred-millionth time she had done that to me. (I was beginning to realize that she did it with everyone she loved.) But that didn't keep the words from stinging—as they always stung. With one little remark, my auntie had managed once more to fill my cup with criticism.

Do you know somebody like that, who seems to delight in pouring doses of criticism? If you don't, just wait a little bit, and one will almost certainly come knocking at your door. Your critic may even be ringing your doorbell or calling you on the phone right now. Someone you just can't please. Someone who excels in bowling over your confidence with just a word or a look.

It may be direct, overt, controlling:

"You shouldn't pick up the baby when he cries."

"I'm afraid blue just isn't your color."

"Thank you, but it's just not our style. I know you won't mind if I return it."

Or it may be more subtle—a backhanded compliment or just a calculating sniff and a martyred look:

"You're so patient. If my children acted like that I'd be mortified."

"Well, yes, I suppose so…"

But no matter how the criticism is poured, the message is clear. You did it wrong. Your efforts just don't measure up. You just aren't good enough... smart enough...pretty enough.

It's so hard to live freely and creatively and lovingly with that kind of criticism. It's hard to risk flying high when you're always afraid of being shot down. I know, because my critical auntie had been pouring out caustic cupfuls for me ever since I could remember.

It wasn't that she didn't care about me. In fact, she had always made it clear that I was special to her. But my auntie's critical spirit led her to express her love with constant attempts to control and change me. From the time I was small, nothing about me had ever been quite right for her—my hair, my speech, my manners, my clothes, my children, or anything else.

And how did I respond?

For years, I just tried harder.

I spent so much of my life in a constant struggle to live up to my aunt's impossible standards.

I would visit the hairdresser and have my nails done before a visit. She would give me the number of *her* hairdresser and manicurist.

I would scour the stores for just the right birthday gift. She would return it.

I would choose my words and my grammar with care, trying so hard not to say anything wrong. She would still find something to criticize.

And then it finally hit me.

All my life I had been holding out my cup to my auntie, waiting for her to fill it with encouragement and praise. And she couldn't do it! Her own cup was too full of a critical spirit to pour anything different into mine. Holding up a bigger or better or more beautiful cup wasn't going to make any difference. And Satan was still using her poured-out criticism to make me feel inadequate and insecure and thus damage my ability to share Christ's love.

If I wanted my cup to hold anything other than criticism, I needed to stop holding it out to my auntie so trustingly. When she poured the criticism in anyway—as she was bound to do—I needed to take what I could learn from her critical words and then dump the bitter brew down the drain.

But it wasn't enough just to empty my cup. If I did, my aunt or someone else would fill it up again. What I needed to do was to keep my cup filled with love and acceptance and affirmation and encouragement from a dependable Source. I had to decide who I wanted to listen to—who was going to have power over me. And making that decision is what would enable me to empty out the criticism, wash out the cup, and then get it refilled from God's bubbling bounty of encouragement.

That, gradually, was what I learned to do. But it didn't happen all at once. It took a lot of time and practice and prayer. That particular painful afternoon, God and I had already been working on this process of emptying and filling for several years.

What did I do in response to her criticism?

I thanked my aunt for the idea. (I hadn't worn a padded bra since high school.) Then I pictured myself slowly turning over that cup of criticism and pouring it out, wiping it clean, holding it up again. And I prayed, *Please, Lord, fill my cup with your love. Let me respond to her criticism with gentleness. Even though she fills my cup with criticism, let me fill her cup with encouragement.*

And, please, Lord, I added, *don't ever let me act like that to others. Teach me to see and express only what is good and healthy in my friends and family.*

How often, I wonder, have I filled others' cups with my criticism by stressing the negative and not focusing on the positive? Whether I liked it or not, I was trained by an expert to look at others with a critical eye. And when your cup is full of criticism, it's so easy to let it overflow into the cups of those around you! That's another reason it's so important that I keep emptying the cup of criticism and filling it with positive things—so I can fill others' cups with encouragement instead of criticism.

First Peter 3:4 reminds us of the importance of cultivating the "inner self, the unfading beauty of a gentle and quiet spirit, which is of great worth in

God's sight" (NIV). That's what I want for my life—a cup of encouragement and affirmation rather than a cup of criticism.

Yet even as I write this, I realize I may have fallen into being critical toward my critical aunt! Yes, she had her faults. But I truly believe she did the best she could with what she was given. And she had so many good qualities. She gave generously to those in need and to many who were not in need. She modeled hard work, rigorous honesty, and the nurturing of family connections. (Until she died, she regularly sent money to our extended family in Romania.) She left me so much—not only her material possessions, but also a heritage of helping others. As I empty my cup of criticism, I want to fill it with encouragement and affirmation and also with gratitude for this woman who loved me and shaped me.

There is so much about any person that is good and beautiful. So focusing on the positive doesn't mean being naive or unrealistic or blind. It simply means learning to accept myself and others for what we are—human beings with faults and good points and also the capacity to grow.

It also means I'm learning to accept the fact that I'm not the one in charge of the universe. It's not my job to change everybody or even to enlighten the world about its problems! Besides, criticism hardly ever changes anybody—except to make the criticized person more angry, resentful, stubborn, and, perhaps, critical of others.

Now, I am not saying we should never speak with one another about problems. I am not saying we should blind ourselves to faults or ignore difficulties. I am not saying we should always sit on our opinions and bite our tongues. And I am certainly not saying we should never return gifts or give our honest opinion about how someone's hair looks.

There is a difference between honest discussion and hurtful accusation. There is a difference between being aware of someone's faults and shattering that person's confidence. There is a big difference between tactfully returning a gift or stating an opinion and filling someone's cup with criticism.

But discerning that difference may involve some honest self-evaluation. A critical spirit can be easy to rationalize, especially in the name of honesty or helpfulness. When there's doubt, I truly believe it's better not to say anything.

So, is your cup filled with criticism?

Are you holding onto your cup and filling the cups of others with the bitter brew?

If you think that's possible, I urge you to stop and pour out your cup of criticism before it poisons you and the people you love. Then begin the work of cleaning out the hurts in your life that make you critical of others.

When criticism starts to fill your cup again, and it will, recognize it for what it is and stop letting it in. Instead, make a point of pouring beauty and love into your cup and the cups of others. Look for something to admire in yourself and others and make a point of expressing that admiration.

If that's hard, think again. We are all children of God, created by him. He made us each beautiful in his sight. Make the effort to find that beauty in yourself and others.

I'm not saying it's easy—the habit of criticism can be deeply ingrained. My auntie remained critical of me until the day she died, and I'm sure I have moments when the old poisonous brew drips from my cup into someone else's.

But the cycle of criticism really can be broken. This is how it works:

First, you examine your cup. You take a tiny sip to see if there's something there you need—some truth you need to hear, even in that unpleasant form. Then you turn your cup, dump out that poisonous draft, and hold out your cup to be filled with God's love and acceptance and encouragement.

And you do it again, repeating the process whenever the criticism begins to flow. Better yet, you keep your cup so full of good things that there's no room for the biting, critical words.

You can do that, you know, because the Lord is

always there for you, waiting to fill your cup with encouragement and affirmation, waiting mercifully to restore your soul when it has been shriveled by criticism. He does it through the words of Scripture, through the soft whisper of his Holy Spirit, and especially through the people who love and accept and support you.

Surely I wouldn't have been able to cope with my auntie's criticism if there hadn't been people who kept my cup brimming with encouragement and affirmation. But God has filled my cup generously through these special people in my life.

I think of my mother, who always believed in me and excelled at the gentle art of teaching without criticizing.

Or I think of my husband, Bob, whose ongoing affirmation has lifted me higher than I ever imagined, and my children and grandchildren, who encourage me in a hundred ways.

Mentors such as Florence Littauer lovingly badgered me into becoming a speaker and a writer when I had no idea I had anything to say or any gift for saying it.

My special friends, who know me so well and love me anyway, give me daily encouragement to keep on.

And I am profoundly grateful to all the hundreds of women who read my books and attend my seminars and then call or write to let me know that God has touched their lives through me.

If God, who knows me more intimately than even Bob or my mother, can use me as a channel of his blessings—and make no mistake, he uses you, too!—then how can I let my cup remain full of criticism? How can I not be encouraged when I remember that God has not only accepted me, but wants to use me to do his work in the world?

That is not to say that everything about me is acceptable to God! In fact, the Scriptures make it clear that I am always falling short of the mark. I never get it all right, no matter how hard I try. No one does.

But here's the amazing lesson for those of us whose cup of criticism has too often been full.

God himself, when confronted with the enormity of human sin, didn't respond by criticizing us. He didn't sit up there in heaven and harp about the way we humans manage to mess up every good thing he ever made.

What he did was become a human being and live among us.

And there's more.

Of all the people on earth, there has been only One with the right and the power to criticize any other human. There has only been One without sin, one person worthy to throw stones at others. And he didn't do it.

What he did was die for us. And that fact alone is enough to fill my cup to overflowing.

But there's more to the story about my critical auntie.

Less than three years after my niece's wedding reception, this same aunt lay dying in her hospital bed. She was eighty-eight. She had fought death to the end with the same determination she had brought to the rest of her life. But now she was very tired, and we knew the end was near.

I remember the last evening in particular. Darkness had already fallen by the time I arrived at the hospital, and the soft lighting in my auntie's room contrasted with the harsh lights of the corridor.

"Your auntie has been very peaceful today," the woman in the next bed told me in her soft Jamaican accent. She was a very sick woman herself, going blind with diabetes. We had gotten to know her a little during the past few days.

I looked at my auntie. Maybe she did look peaceful, compared to her hard days of fighting. But she was so clammy and thin and the color had gone from her and her breathing was so heavy. And as I sat there beside her I began to think back over the years, about the time she had spent with me and the gifts she had given me and also about all the pain she had brought to my life. Somehow it all seemed minor now.

So I put my arms around my auntie, and I put my hankie to her brow, and I began to recite the Twenty-third Psalm, "The Lord is my shepherd, I shall not want...."

And then the soft voice from the next bed was joining in, reciting with me. "He maketh me to lie down in green pastures: he leadeth me beside the still waters. He restoreth my soul..." (KJV).

In the silence of the bare room that sweet Jamaican woman and I recited the familiar words of the psalm. We finished, and then we recited it again, and it was as if angels were hovering in the room.

And now, I thought, my aunt really did look peaceful—or perhaps the peace was in my heart. I pulled the covers up and I tucked her in, and I left. That was the last time I was able to look into my auntie's face, her eyes, and hold her hand, because she died a very few moments after that.

I later found out that the woman in the next bed, a brilliant woman who spoke five languages, had learned the Twenty-third Psalm as a little girl and recited it every night before she went to sleep. What a blessing she was to me in those difficult hours. How she filled my cup with encouragement!

I truly do not know where my auntie is now. Unlike my mother, who came to know Jesus in her later years, my Jewish auntie died without acknowledging the Messiah.

But I do know that the last words she heard were God's Word, and her last human contact was a loving embrace. And I know that happened only because I, by God's grace, had learned to empty out my cup of criticism. God's great and amazing mercy to me during that difficult time was the gift of powerful acceptance and prayer for this woman who had hurt me so deeply, but who also loved me so much. And, oh, how that beautiful gift helped to restore my soul.

Some Words for a Discouraged Heart

PROVERB 3:27
Do not withhold good from those to whom it is due, when it is in the power of your hand to do so.

MARK 14:4-6
But there were some who were indignant among themselves, and said, "Why was this fragrant oil wasted? For it might have been sold for more than three hundred

denarii and given to the poor." And they criticized her sharply. But Jesus said, "Let her alone. Why do you trouble her? She has done a good work for Me."

Romans 8:1

There is therefore now no condemnation to those who are in Christ Jesus, who do not walk according to the flesh, but according to the Spirit.

1 Thessalonians 5:14

Now we exhort you, brethren, warn those who are unruly, comfort the fainthearted, uphold the weak, be patient with all.

1 Peter 4:8-9

And above all things have fervent love for one another, for "love will cover a multitude of sins." Be hospitable to one another without grumbling.

It's Too Much, Lord!

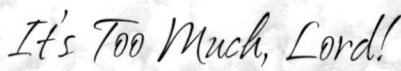

It's too much, Lord!
Just one thing after another—
Too much pain, too much worry,
Too much sadness,
Too many hard days and endless nights,
And I'm just so tired…
Lord, it's just too much.
Help!

8

God Heals Weary Hearts

*God is my strength and power, and He makes
my way perfect.*
—2 Samuel 22:33

It was three o'clock in the afternoon on a day in early December. The chairs for our holiday seminar were being set up in the assembly hall. Our boxes and baskets of prayer planners and feather dusters and rubber "spootulas" were stacked behind the long tables, ready to be displayed and sold. Someone was on the stage, fiddling with the sound system. Someone else was putting up signs.

And me? I was in the process of coming unglued. Dissolving into tears. Totally losing it.

Now, hysterics are not normal for me, especially not right before a seminar. But I was drained from weeks of traveling, doing workshop after workshop in a series of different cities and churches. I was run-down from meeting people, giving to people, hauling books, and making bookings, and I was fighting a low-grade sinus infection that refused to go away. But I had really been looking forward to this seminar because it was here in our very own town, in our very own church, arranged for by people I knew and loved. This one was going to be easy and fun.

Then the woman in charge of the registration process called with a problem. Apparently we had overbooked the hall. Twelve hundred women had sent in their registration forms, and we had seats for only a thousand. The fire marshal had said no to putting in more chairs, so we would have to turn two hundred women away.

That little piece of bad news did it. My composure collapsed like a blob of warm jelly. All I could think of was those two hundred women.

"We can't turn them away," I sobbed. "God moved their hearts to want to come here; he must have a blessing for them. We can't turn them away from getting a blessing. Maybe there's somebody who really needs to be here tonight. We can't turn anybody away. We just can't..."

Without a word our friend Ellen, who helped us in our office and at our seminars, stepped close and took me in her arms. She pressed my head against her shoulder and murmured the way you do to a baby who is out of control.

"There, there, it's going to be all right."

And you know what? It was all right.

Ellen was God's strength to me at that moment. I leaned on her until I calmed down and regained control. Meanwhile, someone stepped in and began making plans for handling the overflow. Seats were found for the extra two hundred people. We even were able to accommodate two women from Oregon who just happened to walk in—although they literally had to sit in the bathroom and watch the seminar on closed-circuit TV.

I completed that weekend with an unusual sense of fulfillment and blessing. Not only did I sense God's presence in a special way during the sessions, but I was also profoundly grateful to Ellen and the others for ministering to me in a moment when life was just too much. And I was reminded in a vivid way of a truth I often want to ignore:

I don't have to be strong all the time.

In fact, God doesn't *want* me to be strong—at least not the way the world usually defines it.

God wants me to learn to lean on him the way I leaned on Ellen, the way a weary shepherd leans on his staff. He wants me to be comforted by his mighty power and to depend on him, not my jerky little efforts, to get through my life. He wants to fill my cup with the strong brew of his magnificent presence.

This is not a new insight. You've probably heard it before. You've heard that the Lord's strength is made perfect in weakness. It is. But what does that mean in terms of how we act and speak in our everyday lives?

Does God want us to *try* to be weak just so he can be strong?

No, that's not it at all. The point is not trying to be weak. The point is that we *are* weak.

We are cracked teacups, crumbling little earthenware creations, made in the divine image and gifted by God, but still weak, subject to breakage. We live in bodies that can break down. We are lazy, inconstant, stained with sin and selfishness, vulnerable to hate and pride and jealousy.

And God?

He is God! He is the creator of the universe, the One who keeps the galaxies whirling. He is the One who dreamed up blue whales and plankton, quantum physics and nuclear energy—and us. He was the One who opened the sea and raised Lazarus from the dead and then conquered death once and for all.

The simple little children's song sums it up succinctly:

Little ones to him belong,

They are weak but he is strong.

So the real issue here is not trying to be weak or strong, but getting a clear view of who we are and who God is.

The Bible doesn't tell us, "Be strong." And it doesn't tell us, "Be weak."

It tells us, "Look at who you are, and look at who God is." And then do the logical thing—which is to lean on him, to depend on his strength.

But it's not always easy to do. We are too brainwashed by the messages of the world: Be tough, get physical, command respect, don't let anyone walk all over you.

We're driven by fear, too. If we're not strong, we think, others will walk all over us. If we're not tough, we won't survive. We need our shell. We need our cocky confidence.

But here's another amazing paradox.

When we try to be strong on our own, we only end up showing how weak we really are. We become stiff and brittle or out of control. Even if we end up on top, we will eventually be toppled.

But when we take an alternate path, God's path, and let him be the strong one, an amazing thing happens. We admit our weakness and lean on him. And then…we become stronger.

I become a strong woman of God when I offer him my cup of weakness and ask him in all humility to fill it with his strength. What an incredible thought: The power that runs the universe is available to me if I am humble enough to accept it.

How do I experience that power? It depends on the situation.

First, God gives me strength to keep going during those times—like that memorable holiday seminar—when my strength gives out. This is almost like spiritual first aid. God may have a lesson for me to learn in the incident, or he may be telling me I need to slow down or make a change. But in the meantime, he often lends me an infusion of strength to carry me through.

Often the strength comes through other people. Ellen was God's strength to me in those awful moments before the holiday seminar. And my Bob has consistently been a source of strength to me in the course of our life together. I especially appreciate his strength and support after I've been on the platform all day and given out everything I know to give. When I feel that all my energy has been drained from my cup, that my strength is totally depleted, Bob will step in to pack up the materials and load the van and take me to dinner. Often he'll carry the conversation or just sit in silence because he understands that I'm all "talked out."

Bob does so much for me that I've always thought of him as "the strong one." But I've begun to realize that Bob and I take turns being strong for each other.

I've seen this with special clarity in the past few years, as we have struggled to cope with painful events in our family. We have rarely been weak at the same time. When Bob is really upset and doesn't feel he can tolerate what's going on, I seem to be handling the situation better or praying more consistently or keeping on a more even keel. Then, when I've had all I can take, Bob will be holding steady.

This is a natural rhythm. I've seen it work with employees in a business and with children in a family. And it works with non-Christians as well as Christians. But I think it is a rhythm God uses to help us. We take turns being God's strength to one another as we care for the people we love.

But God doesn't just work through loved ones in providing the infusions of strength I need to move forward. I've found he can be amazingly creative in supplying me with strength I need. I've had acquaintances or even strangers call me and say, "I'm not sure why I'm calling you, but I want you to know I'm praying for you." Sometimes when that has happened I hadn't even realized I had a need! But other times I knew exactly what the problem was. What a blessing to hear over the phone, "I don't need to know what you're going through; I just really feel that you need some strength from me."

But God's strength is not available just for crisis times. It is also available for my everyday life, for those ordinary days and weeks when nothing much seems to be happening. In those times I need strength to honor my commitments, to do what I ought to do, to keep from being worn down in the daily grind.

This kind of strength comes to me most dependably in my daily communion with God. When I am spending time in the Word and leaning on him in daily prayer, I am also growing stronger. Not only am I better able to handle my ordinary life today, I am also better equipped for tomorrow's crisis.

I find it works a little like that wonderful fabric stiffener you can buy in craft stores. The stiffener is used for making fabric bows that hold their shape without wilting—wonderful for decorating baskets and floral arrangements. To make a bow, you take a strip of fabric and soak it in the thick liquid until all the fibers have been permeated. Then you shape the bow and allow it to dry. The finished product is sturdy and flexible; bows made through this process are beautiful and shapely, and they don't sag or fray.

My times of communion with God work like that stiffener in my life. They soak the fibers of my being in the Lord's strength. When I spend time in prayer and meditation, when I read his Word or read what others have written about him, when I sing or praise or just try to spend time in his presence, I am soaking him up. In myself, I'm still that limp old cotton fabric. But when I have been permeated by him I have the capacity to be strong and resilient and beautiful.

But there's more to living in the Lord's strength than just "soaking" in Scripture and prayer. The actual process of becoming strong and beautiful takes a bit more energy. Growing strong in the Lord is not usually just a matter of sitting around and waiting until I'm strong so that *then* I can do what he wants me to do. More often, it's a matter of doing what I think God wants me to do, trusting that I will be given the strength I need when I need it.

In other words, God doesn't expect me to be strong.

But he does expect me to be obedient.

And I have to say yes to his leading if I want to be a strong woman of God.

I have to follow up on the little nudges and the big messages he has sent me in my prayer times and during the day. I have to step forward, trusting that the Lord who gave the orders will also provide the strength to carry them out.

And that, in turn, takes courage.

It takes courage to say yes to being weak, courage to say yes to the Lord's leading instead of depending on your own strength, courage to say, "I can't do it, Lord. But I'll still try if you go with me."

I have learned that the most amazing infusions of God's strength happen like that, when I am taking the risk of obeying God. So often in my life I have been astonished at how my Lord can take a tiny faith step and turn it into a strong leap for his kingdom.

It's a little like those moving sidewalks in a big airport.

These days, it seems that Bob and I spend half our lives in airports, so we loved this image, which came from my friend Anne's prayer group. (One of the group members even wrote a country-western song about it!)

Picture yourself walking down the concourse, lugging your shoulder bags and dragging your rolling cart behind you. Your boss has sent you on a special assignment, and your gate is at the very end of an impossibly long corridor. But just up ahead you spot the long black walkway with the handrails. It's the moving sidewalk.

A woman just a few paces ahead of you steps on. She's obviously very weak and weary, so she just grabs onto the handrail and lets the walkway carry her along.

Right after her is a businessman with no luggage but a briefcase. He's obviously not in a hurry. So he just steps onto the sidewalk and moves along at a regular pace. But the momentum of the moving panel does add an extra bounce to his step. You can tell because he's passing the people who decided not to take the walkway.

You don't have the leisure of a stroll down the

concourse. You have a mission to accomplish, and you're already walking as fast as you can. Without slowing your pace, you take a big step onto the walkway. And whoosh! you feel the power. Now every step feels like a giant step, taken with less effort. You feel like you're in an old-fashioned sneaker commercial, running faster and jumping higher. The steps are yours, but the walkway is carrying you, too.

I often have that "whoosh" feeling when I step on a platform to speak. I am always in awe of the responsibility I have to the women in my audiences. And there are times when I am so weak, when I feel I don't have the energy to connect even with God. But I am convinced that this is where God wants me, so I go ahead and step on the platform. And in a matter of moments the Spirit of God will take over and strengthen me and give me the power I need to share myself and my Lord.

It doesn't always happen that way. Sometimes I feel pretty energetic and strong, and I may decide to go it on my own. I may decide to skip the moving sidewalk and just walk down the concourse myself. And sometimes I guess I do a pretty good job that way. But it's completely different when I'm relying on the Lord's strength, depending on him to do what needs to be done. I can almost feel the moment when I lean on the Lord and let his strength take over. Whoosh!

And although I've seen it again and again, I'm always amazed at what happens next. I will look out and see every eye glued on me, every ear tuned to the words coming out of my mouth. Sometimes I'll see tears running down cheeks. And then I'll think, "But this is just me—an ordinary housewife and mother with a high school education and a dysfunctional background and no training in speaking or writing. What am I doing here that would be so meaningful to them?"

I really am not trying to put myself down here. I know that God has made me special. But I also know that what happens in those seminars is so far beyond what I am capable of on my own that I can't take any of the credit. It's God's strength and the power of his Word coming through.

And that power and strength is available to you, no matter what your life is like, whether you're at the end of your rope or just moving along in an ordinary life or ready to take a big, risky step into ministry of some kind. The promise of God's strength doesn't apply just to speakers or writers or ministers. I have seen him at work in so many different lives, seen the amazing things that result when men and women give him their weakness and rely on his strength.

I think of a woman I know who has suffered emotional problems to the point of being in and out of mental hospitals. I can't imagine coping with the kind of pain she has endured. And yet she keeps moving forward, keeps holding out her cup to receive the Lord's strength. She uplifts me.

Or I think of a friend whose only daughter has struggled with dyslexia, has had an abortion, has attempted suicide. My friend has agonized, worried, intervened. She has also had to cope with losing a house and with ongoing financial instability. Yet this is the friend who has taught me how to crawl up into the lap of my heavenly Father and find strength in his arms. She teaches me how to find strength in weakness.

I think of my strong Bob, who touches the lives of so many women in our seminars because he is willing to be open and vulnerable to them, to be honest about his feelings and weaknesses. He even lets me talk about him in my seminars—a position of weakness that requires enormous strength and courage. I have always loved and respected my Bob, but my respect has grown as I have observed his willingness to be weak in the Lord's service and have watched him grow stronger in the Lord's love.

I think of so many other people—young moms with children at home, dads whose teenagers are in trouble, people struggling with illness or working at jobs that sap their spirits. And these men and women are an example to me because I see them turning to the Lord in their pain and weakness. Turning to him when life seems too much or just too daily, or when the challenge is beyond them.

The simple child's song really is true.

We *are* weak.

But he *is* strong.

And his mighty arms are outstretched to us, ready to pour out his strength into our weak and fragile little cups.

And all we have to do is hold them up to him.

Some Words for a Weary Heart

ISAIAH 40:29-31

He gives power to the weak, and to those who have no might He increases strength. Even the youths shall faint and be weary, and the young men shall utterly fall, but those who wait on the LORD shall renew their strength; they shall mount up with wings like eagles, they shall run and not be weary, they shall walk and not faint.

2 Corinthians 12:9

My grace is sufficient for you, for My strength is made perfect in weakness.

Exodus 15:2

The Lord is my strength and song, and He has become my salvation; He is my God, and I will praise Him; my father's God, and I will exalt Him.

Psalm 29:11

The Lord will give strength to His people; the Lord will bless His people with peace.

Psalm 116:6-7

The Lord preserves the simple; I was brought low, and He saved me. Return to your rest, O my soul, for the Lord has dealt bountifully with you.

Matthew 11:28-30

Come to Me, all you who labor and are heavy laden, and I will give you rest. Take My yoke upon you and learn from Me, for I am gentle and lowly in heart, and you will find rest for your souls. For My yoke is easy and My burden is light.

How Much Longer, Lord?

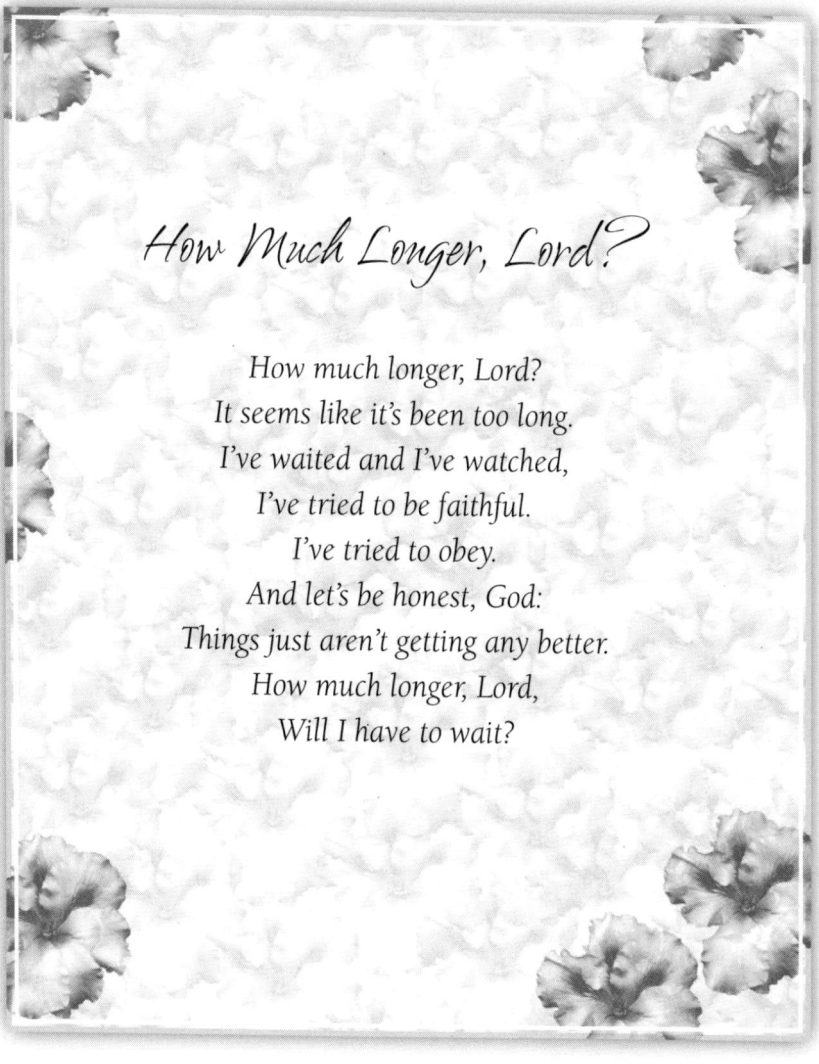

How much longer, Lord?
It seems like it's been too long.
I've waited and I've watched,
I've tried to be faithful.
I've tried to obey.
And let's be honest, God:
Things just aren't getting any better.
How much longer, Lord,
Will I have to wait?

9

God Heals Impatient Hearts

*I wait for the LORD, my soul waits, and in his
word I put my hope.*
—PSALM 130:5 NIV

I thought it would take three months.

I thought it would transform my daughter's life.

And I was right on both counts, except that it didn't happen at all the way I thought.

The way it did happen, though, taught me some important things about prayer...and waiting.

When my daughter Jenny first walked out on her husband and her marriage and her God in February of 1994, I was distraught. I was furious at Jenny for leaving. I was desperately worried for my daughter's three children. I ached for my son-in-law and worried for my husband's health as I saw him agonize over the situation.

But what could I do? How could I help?

That month, I was scheduled to speak at the Southern California Woman's Retreat. Reluctantly, and without giving any details, I shared a little of my pain and worry with the women at that retreat. And afterwards, a woman came up to me and said, "I know a book that can help you." She said, "I've had difficulties with my daughter, too. But then I found this little book called *Praying God's Will for My Daughter*. It's really Scripture arranged into topics, and it can help you to pray God's Word over your daughter. I did that, and in three months my daughter's life began to change."

"That sounds really good to me," I said. I've always believed in disciplined, focused prayer, and this book sounded like just what I needed. I really wanted God's will for Jenny. I was positive that the reuniting of that family was God's will! And three months—that wasn't so long to change a person's life. I could do this for Jenny. I *wanted* to do it.

So I went to a Christian bookstore and found the little book the woman had mentioned, *Praying God's Will for My Daughter* by Lee Roberts. In the front of the book was this promise:

If you follow a systematic plan of praying God's will for your daughter, you will see dynamic growth take place in her life. She will become the person God intended her to be.

In my heart, that's what I wanted most of all. I brought that little book home and began to take it along with me to the canal path where I take my daily walk. For those forty-five minutes every day I used that book to help me pray God's Word over my daughter.

The day I began, I marked the date in the front of the book. I started at the beginning, with the topic of anger, and I prayed from Ephesians as it directed:

God, in accordance with Your Word, I pray that Jenny will let all bitterness, wrath, anger, clamor, and evil speaking be put away from her, with all malice. I pray also that she will be kind to others, tenderhearted, forgiving others, just as God in Christ forgave her.

That was the beginning.

Each day I would lace up my tennis shoes, drive to the canal path, walk, and read from that little Scripture book. Each day I would cry, and cry to God, on behalf of my confused, hurting daughter.

Weeks passed. I worked my way from the topics of "Anger" and "Attitude" all the way through to "Worried." I reached the end of the book. Nothing had changed.

Some things take time, I reminded myself.

So I wrote the date in the back of the book and started over.

Three months had passed. The woman at the retreat had said her daughter was changed in three months, but nothing seemed different about our Jenny. She was still angry, still alienated from church, still dating men who were no good for her, still not paying enough attention (as I saw it) to her children. She showed no signs of repenting for her actions or returning to her husband.

Oh well, I sighed. *I guess God has a little harder job to do on my daughter than on this other lady's daughter!*

So I kept on walking and praying. I wrote another "finished" date in the back of the book, and then another. And one day I happened to look at those dates and I realized I had been praying God's Word over Jenny for an entire year!

That day I had been reading the Scriptures under the topic of "Trust." And as I pondered God's words on trust I suddenly realized I was weeping.

"God, I *have* trusted you," I blurted out, "and you're not *doing* anything; nothing is happening. I don't see any change in Jenny. I don't see that she's back with her husband. I trusted you for the healing of this family, I've prayed for that, and it just hasn't happened."

I stalked on down the path, pumping my arms hard in my frustration. I walked another quarter mile, then another. And then, in the depths of my heart, I seemed to hear God's answer:

Emilie, trust me, he whispered in my heart. *I know the beginning from the end.*

"God, I'm *trying* to trust you," I shot back, "but

you're not making it easy! You haven't *done* anything."

And still I seemed to hear, echoing deeply: *Trust me, trust me, trust me.*

So I walked a little further, reached the end of the path, and quietly headed for my car. I finally shrugged my shoulders and said, "All right, God, I want to trust you, but you've got to help me."

So I kept up my routine of walking and praying for Jenny from that little Scripture book. But now, in addition, whenever I would think about the situation during the day, I would pray, "God, I want to trust you. Please help me to trust you."

The situation still didn't change. I worked my way through the little book again, and again. But gradually, over time, I realized I was finding it a little easier to trust God for my daughter…and then even a little easier.

Something was changing, *something*, although it wasn't what I wanted in the first place. Quietly, gently, my faith was growing.

Another six months passed, then another three. One day I was reading in the section on forgiveness and praying, as I often did, that I would be able to forgive Jenny for what she had done to our family. In the past weeks, God had been showing me just how angry I was with her for hurting us all with her actions.

"Dear Lord," I prayed. "I know you want me to forgive her. Please help."

And then I was surprised to hear God saying in my heart: *Emilie, you need to ask Jenny to forgive you.*

That stopped me cold. "Ask her forgiveness for what? What have *I* done to *her*? She's the one who walked out on her family."

But then as I went on to read those Scriptures on forgiveness, I began to see the answers. I also realized that I really did want to be obedient to God. And so that afternoon I called my daughter and said, "Jenny, I need to come over and talk to you."

Now, Jenny knew I had been praying the Word of God over her. So she was not really surprised when I told her what I had been reading. But she was very surprised when I said, "Jenny, please, will you forgive me? I've resented you. I've blamed you. I've been critical of you. And I'm sorry. Please forgive me for what I've said and done."

Then I left. Jenny hardly said anything—I suppose she was in shock! But two days later I received a lovely note that said, "Mom, I love you. And I do forgive you."

It was only after that that I began to see the little changes in my Jenny's life. I began to see her Bible come out. Then, all of a sudden, she was going to church again, and she took the children on the weekends when they were with her. She was talking with them and communicating better. She was going to a counselor and getting some help with her own needs. Things were definitely getting better.

But Jenny still didn't go back to her husband. She didn't want to even think about it. My grandchildren still suffered from their broken home.

And then one day as I was walking and praying, I came to the Scripture that says we're to be thankful in all things. I thought I heard God saying: *Emilie, I want you to thank me.*

And I said, "Lord, I really am thankful for the changes I'm seeing in Jenny. So thank you."

Then the Lord spoke again in my heart: *I want you to thank me for all of it.*

"But how can I do that, Lord? How can I be thankful for the pain or the separation? (At this point, no one had filed for divorce.) How can I be thankful that my precious grandchildren's hearts are broken?"

And the answer came: *I want you to thank me today for what I will do tomorrow.*

I shook my head. I honestly didn't think I could do it. I felt like a hypocrite even trying. But I still wanted to be obedient to God, and so I did begin to thank him—for what had happened in the past, for what was happening at present, for what would happen in the future.

By this time, though, nearly three years had

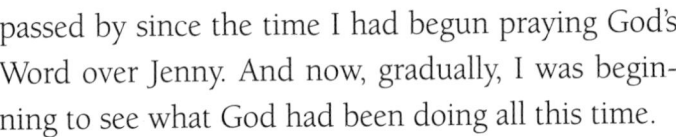

passed by since the time I had begun praying God's Word over Jenny. And now, gradually, I was beginning to see what God had been doing all this time.

You see, I was praying for God to change Jenny.

But what God was really doing was changing *me*.

Day after day, step by step, through the Scripture-prayers I had been reading on Jenny's behalf, God had been pouring his heart into mine. Step by step, word by word, I was being restored and supported and strengthened and established, being given what I would need not only to support my family, but also to face the ongoing health problems that were now beginning to reach a crisis level in my life.

Trust me, he had said. And I was learning to trust that God was in charge and would accomplish what needed to be accomplished.

Forgive and be forgiven, he had said. And I was seeing vivid confirmation of what a dramatic change forgiveness could bring about.

Thank me, he had said. And my dutiful thanks were beginning to be heartfelt thanks…even for the new trials I was going through.

I didn't stop walking and praying for my daughter. In my heart, day by day, I could feel the trust and the forgiveness and the gratitude growing.

And then one day in October, after I had been praying for my Jenny more than three and a half years, I answered my phone to hear her crying hysterically. "Mom, I need you right now," she said. I live only a few miles away, and so I was soon at her door.

Her face was still streaked with tears as she led me to a chair. "Mom," she said, "I've been battling with God for three days now. And I've been reading the Word of God over and over and over again. And I truly believe God is telling me to go back home to my husband. I think I'm supposed to do whatever it takes...counseling, marriage therapy, whatever...to make it work."

And then she said, "Mom, I really want to be obedient to God, so I'm going to do that."

I was stunned and amazed. By this time, Jenny had been dating someone steadily, a good man she really enjoyed. Her husband also had a girlfriend. The divorce papers had been filed. Jenny had gone to a counselor and worked hard on beginning a new life. And now she was telling me that being obedient to God was more important to her than this new life she was starting.

Now I really had something to be thankful for. To see my child growing in love and obedience to her heavenly Father—that was all I had ever truly wanted for her. That afternoon she and I cried together and prayed together and read the Word together. And a day or two later she went to her husband and asked him to forgive her and promised to do whatever it took to make their family whole again.

I wish I could tell you that Jenny's husband welcomed her with open arms and that their family is back together again.

Sadly, it didn't happen that way.

Rather than taking Jenny back when she asked, her husband said it was too late. He was already involved with someone else. He couldn't put the hurt behind him. He had no interest in rebuilding their relationship.

And so the actual, physical ending to this story has not been what I wanted it to be. But the words in the front of that little book of Scripture have indeed come true. In the past year I *have* seen dynamic growth in my daughter's life. I have seen her move closer to being the person God intended her to be. God is doing a strengthening, healing, miraculous work in our lives. When I visit her home and see her praying with the children and reaching out to her neighbors, I marvel at the strong woman of God she has become.

And it all took so much longer than I expected, but that was a mercy, too. The longer I had to wait for God's answer, you see, the more I poured the Word of God into my cup.

And now, more than ever, I understand why it

sometimes seems to take so long for God to accomplish his work in us.

He doesn't have to do things the long way! God is God, and if he wants to zap us with a lightning bolt, he can. He could change our circumstances with the blink of an eye. But I think God is a lot more interested in changing hearts than he is in changing circumstances. And changing a stubborn human heart takes time, even for a sovereign Lord.

And there's another reason I believe God sometimes makes us wait a bit before our prayers are answered and our pain is eased and our dreams come to fruition. So much of the time, God is planning to do so much more with our prayers and our lives than we could ever have envisioned. God sees the big picture, the whole tapestry of the way our lives intertwine with others. Much of the time, when we feel the waiting is intolerable, I believe the Lord of all is making connections and preparing us for the time when we will receive more than we ever asked for.

This has certainly been the case in my prayers for Jenny. For so long, I prayed for things to go back to the way they were. Instead, God has done a beautiful, unexpected work in all our lives. He has given me, in many ways, a new daughter.

I saw a similar, unexpectedly wonderful outworking of God's plan recently. While speaking in northern California, Bob and I became reacquainted with a couple we had known years ago in our church. When we first met them, Kyle and Jeannie had been married eight years. And although they were happy in their jobs (she's a nurse, he's a junior-high basketball coach and an assistant principal), what they wanted more than anything else was a family of their own. But it just wasn't happening. As far as any of us could tell, our prayers for Kyle and Jeannie to have a child were just going unanswered.

By the time Kyle and Jeannie received a job offer in the north and decided to move, they had also decided to try a different path to a family. Not long after their move, we received the news that they had decided to adopt. And instead of adopting an infant, they adopted two little brothers, ages five and seven, who had been in foster homes for years.

Since then, our friends have kept us informed about how their family is doing. The path has not always been smooth! Not surprisingly, those little boys came to Kyle and Jeannie with considerable emotional problems. They had never been taught discipline or manners, and they certainly did not know Christ. The family still struggles to make up for those early years of pain and neglect. But still, the lives of all four are so much better now than any of them ever dreamed.

Kyle and Jeannie wanted a baby. What they got

was the chance to change the lives of two children who needed them desperately.

Those two little boys needed a home. What they got was a mother who was a nurse and could attend to their physical problems, plus an educator father who understood little boys and their needs. Today the boys are in school, and they're learning to work on computers. They can set the table and eat with manners. Best of all, they love Jesus and know the Lord's healing presence in their lives.

What a beautiful, beautiful answer to those prayers we had prayed over those long years—a loving, Christ-centered family, lovingly prepared by our heavenly Father who saw the big picture when all that most of us could see was "Wait."

I hope I can remember that the next time I hear my teeth grinding because God is taking so long to answer my prayers, when I'm ready for results and the only answer I seem to get is "Not yet."

I hope I can remember to trust...because God knows the end from the beginning.

I hope I can remember to keep on forgiving and asking forgiveness, even when I don't feel like doing it...because forgiveness is one of God's most useful tools for changing lives.

I hope I remember to thank him today for what will happen tomorrow...because thankfulness keeps my heart hopeful and open to receiving his blessings.

When my cup is overflowing with trouble and God doesn't seem to be doing anything, I hope I can remember that sometimes the waiting (and the growing) is exactly what I need the most.

Some Words
for an Impatient Heart

1 Thessalonians 1:2-3
We give thanks to God always for you all, making mention of you in our prayers, remembering without ceasing your work of faith, labor of love, and patience of hope in our Lord Jesus Christ in the sight of our God and Father.

Hebrews 6:11-12
And we desire that each one of you show the same diligence to the full assurance of hope until the end, that you do not become sluggish, but imitate those who through faith and patience inherit the promises.

JAMES 1:2-3

My brethren, count it all joy when you fall into various trials, knowing that the testing of your faith produces patience.

JAMES 5:7-8

Therefore be patient, brethren, until the coming of the Lord. See how the farmer waits for the precious fruit of the earth, waiting patiently for it until it receives the early and latter rain. You also be patient. Establish your hearts, for the coming of the Lord is at hand.

PROVERB 19:11

A man's wisdom gives him patience; it is to his glory to overlook an offense.

(NIV)

COLOSSIANS 3:12

Therefore, as God's chosen people, holy and dearly loved, clothe yourselves with compassion, kindness, humility, gentleness and patience.

(NIV)

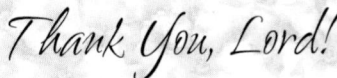

Thank You, Lord!

Thank you, Lord!
When my cup overflowed with trouble,
You made my cup deeper and stronger.
You washed it free of trouble
And filled me to overflowing
With your goodness,
And you keep on doing it
Every day of my life.
You are a God of abundant mercy.
You are a God of abundant strength.
You are a God of abundant blessings.
It's really too much, Lord.
But thank you!

10

Learning to Be Thankful While God Heals Your Heart

Oh, that men would give thanks to the LORD
for His goodness,
And for His wonderful works to the children
of men!
–PSALM 107:31

"For what we are about to receive, the Lord make us truly thankful."

It's a familiar table grace—at least for those of us who still gather around the table at mealtimes and ask a blessing. We say it almost without thinking. It's just one of those standard mealtime prayers—easy to pronounce over a groaning holiday table when loved ones are gathered together.

But have you ever thought of praying that blessing for all the circumstances of your life? Have you ever thought of asking the Lord to give you the gift of gratitude for whatever life has poured into your cup?

That's what I'm trying to learn.

These days I am trying to pray this way on a daily basis.

"Lord, for whatever I am receiving and about to receive—pain as well as joy—please teach me the secret of giving thanks. For what I have already received—what has shaped my life in the past, and what is shaping me today—please fill my cup with thankfulness."

This is not an easy prayer to say with sincerity. In fact, I often feel a little hypocritical when I'm praying it. There are quite a few times in my life when I don't really want to be thankful.

I'm not particularly inclined to be thankful when there is upset and pain in our family. I don't really feel thankful for the chronic pain that some of my friends are suffering in their bodies. I'm certainly not up to offering a heartfelt thanksgiving when I feel like the world and even God have slapped me in the face.

Yes, I know we are supposed to "rejoice always, pray without ceasing, in everything give thanks" (1 Thessalonians 5:16-18). I believe that. But how often do the thank-yous come through gritted teeth? How often have I had to offer thanks because God said so, all the while feeling like a liar?

It's one thing to offer thanks because it's the right thing to do.

It's another thing to be truly thankful.

So how do I do it?

Only by remembering that all things come from God, including our own attitudes. An attitude of thankfulness is a gift God gives to us, a healing libation he pours into our cups. But we must choose to accept it, even to ask for it. Our part is to offer whatever is in our cup to the Lord, and then ask him to fill our cup with true thankfulness.

"For what I am about to receive, the Lord make me truly thankful."

What I am asking for, really, is an attitude adjustment. I am asking for a new way of looking at my life—past, present, and future.

Filling my cup with thankfulness for the past, for instance, means taking a step beyond forgiveness and opening my arms to the circumstances that made me what I am today. It means developing a new attitude toward the people and events that influenced me, even those who treated me ill or meant me harm. It means celebrating the good that God was able to do through those circumstances.

Yes, it's hard, especially for those of us whose childhoods were painful. For a few, filling our cup with gratitude for the past means just being grateful that it's over! But most of us who hold our cup of past pain up to the Lord will find that a thankful attitude can transform even painful memories.

I am finally reaching a place, for example, where

I can honestly thank God for my father and even for the turmoil I experienced while growing up— not because that turmoil was part of God's plan, but because as I look back I can see God working in the midst of it all. As my attitude adjusts into a spirit of thanksgiving, I am able to see beautiful tracings of God's handiwork in my dark memories. For it was the turmoil and insecurity I knew in those days that made me so hungry to know a Father God, that gave me such a yearning for a Savior. Had my Jewish upbringing been happier or more secure, perhaps I would not have embraced the Messiah.

There are many other difficult areas of my past that I am learning to embrace, to see with eyes of gratitude. There may be painful things in your past, too, that need to be redeemed with the eyes of thanksgiving. Or perhaps there are hidden treasures, unappreciated legacies that begin to gleam when viewed in a thankful light.

I'm always amazed, for instance, when women complain to me that they "don't have a testimony" because they grew up in a Christian home. They seem sad or a little embarrassed that they don't have a dramatic story to tell of a radical life-change. It's as if they think they have somehow been robbed of the ability to have an influence for the Lord.

What a devious ploy of Satan—to turn a magnificent, gracious gift into a source of embarrassment! Being raised in a Christian home is a reason for profuse thanksgiving. Scripture, hymns, and Christian attitudes learned early become a fountain of enrichment for all of life. I have to really praise our grandchildren's parents for a good Christian foundation in their school and church. Tears fill my eyes when I see them praying or studying Scripture because I never had that kind of solid spiritual grounding in my young life. Whether or not God gives those children a dramatic "testimony," they will always have the Word of God deep in their hearts. That is good reason to be truly thankful.

But the attitude adjustment of thanksgiving is not just for the past. It's something I need every day in the present, and for the future.

To fill my present cup with thanksgiving means to live in the belief that God is working for good even when things seem to be falling apart.

And I find that harder to do right now than I have at any other time in my life.

The last few years have been difficult ones for our family. I have found it harder to trust God, harder to speak with confidence, harder sometimes even to get through the day. Harder, certainly, to live in thanksgiving. Day to day, my cup has been filled with pain.

And yet that is exactly why I so desperately need the attitude adjustment of thanksgiving. I need it to give meaning to my pain, to redeem it with the reminder of what God has to offer me in my hurtful circumstances.

And what does God give me in my pain? What reason do I have to be thankful?

First of all, he offers the gift of comfort—a significant mercy.

The promise is stark and direct in the King James Version: "I will not leave you comfortless" (John 14:18). Other translations say it differently: "I will not leave you all alone" (TEV), "I will not leave you desolate" (RSV), "I will not leave you as orphans" (NIV). But the message is the same.

You may be hurting, says the Lord, but I will be with you all along the way. If you trust me, I will provide you comfort.

I have been comforted profoundly at times, in the very center of my pain, by a simple sense of God's presence, the nearness of the Holy Spirit. I can come to him and simply lean on him, drawing comfort from his nearness. Sometimes I pray, sharing my troubles and asking for his help. Or sometimes my knees buckle and I sink down wordless in the arms of my heavenly Father. If I pray on a disciplined, consistent basis, my prayer closet is likely the first place I want to go when my cup fills with pain.

And yet there are other times when I need the Lord's comfort in more concrete form. Especially during those times when my faith is weak or my spirit is overwhelmed or my body is failing me, I need God's presence to be incarnated—to take on flesh.

And in those times he brings me comfort in the form of friends who love me and pray for me or simply watch and wait with me.

I will never forget the comfort a friend offered to me in Jesus' name during a time of awful physical pain. I learned later that I had picked up a parasite in my colon. But at the time I knew only that something was making my abdomen hurt. The pain quickly became so bad that I had to excuse myself from a dinner party and lie down. I lay there ten or fifteen minutes, curled up in a fetal position, fearful and hurting. And then my friend Susan came in. She put her arms around me and prayed for me, and I felt that God had sent an angel to comfort me. The pain didn't stop or go away, but it became tolerable. I was able to go home and sleep, and the next day I went to the doctor.

A special source of comfort in times of pain is the companionship of those who have been through the same ordeal. There is a sense of camaraderie and understanding in shared pain, and I believe God uses that fellowship to extend comfort to his children.

Several years ago I broke my foot. I quickly found that while many people were sympathetic, those who had been through the same experience could offer a special kind of comfort because they really understood what I was facing. And now, whenever I see someone with a cast, my empathy and compassion begin to flow. I can honestly say, "I know exactly how that feels, how that pain can shoot, how that foot burns." In the same way, I can resonate with the pain of those who have lost a parent or who have grown up in an alcoholic home. I can offer them a special brand of comfort because I know. I understand.

That doesn't mean, of course, that I can't offer comfort to someone who is going through something I haven't experienced. If I am willing, God can work through me to extend his comfort to anyone in pain, just as he works through others to comfort me. I can offer my presence, my words. I can bring a casserole or volunteer to help with chores. I can offer myself to the Lord as a human expression of his comfort. And I know that he works through such an offering, because I have been on the receiving end. I have been deeply comforted by men and women who showed me the Lord's comfort.

For the Christian there's probably not much else that comforts the soul more than God's Word. I find the psalms especially helpful. They are so honest and direct. They remind me that I am not alone in my pain, and they carry me through my pain to renewed faith. They help me adjust my attitude to one of thanksgiving.

But the most compelling source of comfort I find in Scripture is the reminder that my Lord is no stranger to pain. He chose to become human, to share our pain in order to move us beyond it. He knows what it is like to be rejected, to feel physical discomfort and spiritual desolation, to pray that the cup of pain would be taken away. He knows what agony is like, even what death is like.

But there is more than companionship here. I learn this, too, in the pages of holy Scripture.

My Lord is with me in my pain, but he also is greater than pain, greater than fear, greater even than death. He is with me in the midst of my suffering, but he will also carry me beyond it. If I continue holding up my cup to him, he will do more than fill it, he will also transform it.

This promise of transformation is the second gift our Lord has to offer in my pain. And this is not a consolation prize. This is not a paltry offering I get in return for giving up on earthly happiness. What God promises me in the midst of my pain is real life, real joy, incredible growth, unbelievable beauty.

This is what God has had in mind for me all along. This is what he is doing in the midst of all my circumstances. In the long run, this is "what I am about to receive." I'm going to be changed into something wonderful.

Because I love to collect beautiful teacups and saucers, I love a little parable someone shared with me years ago. I have taken this little tale by an unknown author and retold it in a way that speaks most deeply to me about my own pain and my own transformation.

The story begins in a little gift shop, a charming establishment crammed full of delightful discoveries. A man and a woman have gone there to find a special gift for their granddaughter's birthday. With excited oohs and ahs, they pick up dolls and books and figurines, intent on finding just the perfect piece.

Suddenly, glancing into the corner of an antique armoire, the grandmother spies a prize.

"Oh, honey, look!" she exclaims, taking her husband by the arm and pointing. Carefully he reaches over to pick up the delicate teacup in his big hand. A shaft of sunlight from the window shines through the translucent china, illuminating a delicate design.

"Oh, isn't it pretty?" the grandmother sighs.

He nods, "I don't know much about dishes, but I'd have to say that's the best-looking cup I've ever seen."

Together they gaze at the beautiful little cup, already imagining their granddaughter's face when she opens her special gift. And at that moment something remarkable happens. Something magic.

With a voice as clear and sweet as the painted nosegay on the saucer, that teacup begins to talk.

"I thank you for the compliment," the cup begins. "But you know, I haven't always been like this."

A little shaken at being addressed by a teacup, the grandfather places it back on the shelf and takes a step back. But his wife doesn't seem surprised at all. Instead, she asks with interest, "Whatever are you talking about?"

"Well," says the teacup, "I wasn't always beautiful. In fact, I started out as an ugly, soggy lump of clay. But one day a man with dirty, wet hands started slinging me around, pounding me on a worktable, knocking the breath out of me. I didn't like this procedure one little bit. It hurt, and it made me angry.

" 'Stop!' I cried.

"But the man with the wet hands simply said, 'Not yet!'

"Finally the pounding stopped, and I breathed a sigh of relief. I thought my ordeal was over. But it had just begun.

"The next thing I knew, I was being stuffed into a mold—packed in so tightly I couldn't see straight.

" 'Stop! Stop!' I cried until I was squeezed too tight to utter a sound. Parts of me oozed out of the mold, and he scraped these away.

"If I could have talked, I would have screamed.

"But the man seemed to know what I was thinking. He just looked down with a patient expression on his face and told me, 'Not yet.'

"Finally, the pressing and the scraping stopped. But the next experience was far worse. I was plunged into the dark, and then the temperature began to rise. The air grew hotter and hotter, until I was in agony. I still couldn't talk, but inside I was yelling, 'Get me out of here!'

"And strangely, through those thick furnace walls, I seemed to hear someone saying, 'Not yet.'

"Just when I was sure I was going to be completely incinerated, the oven began to cool. Eventually the man took me out of the furnace and released me from that confining mold. I relaxed. I even looked around and enjoyed my new form. I was firmer. I had shape. This was better.

"But then came the short lady in the smock. She pulled out tiny brushes and began to daub paint all over me. The fumes made me feel sick, and the brush tickled.

"'I don't like that.' I cried. 'I've had enough. Please stop.'

"'Not yet!' said the short lady with a smile.

"Finally she finished. She picked up her brushes and moved on. But just when I thought I was finally free, the first man picked me up again and put me back into that awful furnace. This time was worse than before because I wasn't protected by the mold.

"Again and again I screamed, 'Stop!'

"And each time the man answered through the door of the furnace, 'Not yet!'

"Finally the oven cooled once more, and the man came to open the door. By that time I was almost done in. I barely noticed when I was picked up and put down and packed in a box and jounced and jolted some more. When I finally came to, a pretty lady was picking me up out of my box and placing me on this shelf, next to this mirror.

"And when I looked at myself in the mirror, I was amazed. No longer was I ugly, soggy, and dirty. I was shining and clean. And I was beautiful—unbelievably beautiful. 'Could this be me?' I cried for joy.

"It was then," said the teacup, "that I realized there was a purpose in all that pain. You see, it took all that suffering to make me truly beautiful."

And we can be beautiful, too. That's what God wants for us regardless of the circumstances of our lives.

That doesn't mean that God sends us pain just to test us. I don't believe that God kills off loved ones and tortures innocent children with incurable diseases and turns our friends against us just so that he can teach us a lesson. The God of the New Testament is not a sadistic deity who delights in sending trials just to see if we humans will make it through. He doesn't have to. The human race and the forces of darkness are quite up to the challenge of causing enough pain and suffering and rejection to go around.

And yet our God, through his magnificent powers of redemption, has never lost the upper hand. Whatever ugliness we encounter, whatever suffering we undergo, whatever pain we stumble through, he has the power to redeem it, if we continue to hold up our cups to him.

We can take the pain of our past and the pain of our present and allow that pain to encase us for a lifetime if we want to. But that isn't what God wants us to do. God wants us to bring our cup of pain to him. He wants to comfort us, and he wants to transform us into something beautiful.

And for his loving presence yesterday and today and tomorrow, we can be truly and sincerely thankful.

Some Words for a Heart Learning to Be Thankful

PSALM 30:4-5,10-12

Sing praise to the Lord, you saints of His, and give thanks at the remembrance of His holy name. for His anger is but for a moment, His favor is for life; weeping may endure for a night, but joy comes in the morning....Hear, O Lord, and have mercy on me; Lord, be my helper! You have turned for me my mourning into dancing; You have put off my sackcloth and clothed me with gladness, to the end that my glory may sing praise to You and not be silent. O Lord my God, I will give thanks to You forever.

1 CHRONICLES 16:34

Oh, give thanks to the LORD, for He is good! for His mercy endures forever.

1 THESSALONIANS 5:16-18

Rejoice always, pray without ceasing, in everything give thanks; for this is the will of God in Christ Jesus for you.

1 PETER 1:6-9,13

In this you greatly rejoice, though now for a little while, if need be, you have been grieved by various trials, that the genuineness of your faith, being much more precious than gold that perishes, though it is tested by fire, may be found to praise, honor, and glory at the revelation of Jesus Christ, whom having not seen you love. Though now you do not see Him, yet believing you rejoice with joy inexplicable and full of glory, receiving the end of your faith—the salvation of your souls....

Therefore gird up the loins of your mind, be sober, and rest your hope fully upon the grace that is to be brought to you at the revelation of Jesus Christ.

PSALM 92:1-4

It is good to give thanks to the LORD, and to sing praises to Your name, O Most High; to declare Your lovingkindness in the morning, and Your faithfulness every night, on an instrument of ten strings, on the lute, and on the harp, with harmonious sound. For You, LORD, have made me glad through Your work; I will triumph in the works of Your hands.

Afterword:

The Rest of the Story...So Far

I said at the beginning that there's more to this story.

The years since these books appeared have been both traumatic and deeply fulfilling. In some ways, I wouldn't wish them on anyone. And yet I wouldn't trade them for the world.

The puzzling health problems I describe in this book—recurring bronchitis, a diagnosis of leukemia, a painful ulcer—all turned out to have another, underlying cause. I tell the story of my journey with a rare form of lymphoma in my book, *A Journey Through Cancer.* But the short version is familiar to many—chemotherapy, radiation, blood tests, good news, bad news, and many, many prayers. In my case, the road to healing included a bone marrow transplant and an excruciating six-year battle with shingles. It also involved countless lessons in God's faithfulness and sufficiency.

Today, seven years after the last words of this book were published, I am officially—if cautiously—cancer free. I thank God every day for his ongoing healing of my body and my spirit...and for the skill and generosity of those who contributed to this healing.

I thank God, too, for the love of my family and for their growth during these difficult years. Through it all, my Bob stayed by my side, taking on the bulk of our household responsibilities as well as nursing me, running our business, and even writing more books of his own. He's always been "my Bob," but these days he's truly my hero.

To simplify our lives, we downsized, selling our beloved converted "Barnes Barn" in Riverside, California, and moving closer to my oncologist, who practices in Newport Beach, California. It was hard to leave a place we'd lived for twenty-plus years. But we love our new "Barnes at the Beach" home. These days I take my daily walks in a place I've always loved...by the sea.

I rejoice daily to see the woman our Jenny has become...strong, nurturing, sure of herself and her faith. She is now married to a strong Christian man named Bill, whom we all adore. Her children are almost out of the nest now, in college or building lives of their own. Our son, Brad, is thriving, too, and his adorable sons are the light of our lives.

Though I cut back on speaking and writing during the cancer years, our ministry, More Hours in My Day, continues under the leadership of our partners, Sheri and Tim Torelli. (Visit us at www.emiliebarnes.com.) Sheri is a wonderful speaker and writer who handles most of our seminars. But Bob and I are still speaking, too, on a limited schedule. What a joy to find that, after so many changes in my life, I still have the joy of sharing what I have learned with others.

Which brings me to today, to this moment, when I write this to you. You, me—it's yet another snapshot along the journey of life. I haven't arrived yet—not by a long shot. God is still telling me "Not yet" in certain areas of my life—complications from my cancer, some permanent and painful side effects, lingering personal and family problems, career questions. As I write, we're even having another season of downpours here in southern California! But God is good. I've seen him work too many miracles in my life to doubt that for a minute, and I'm eager to see what he'll do next.

I want you to know that such miracles, little and large, are available for your journey too. In all circumstances of your life—the dry seasons, the muddy ones, the beautiful days at the beach and the years in the desert—he desires your healing, your growth, and most of all your heart. So my final word to you is really his word:

May goodness and mercy follow you all the days of your life.

And may you dwell—may we all dwell—in the Lord's house forever.

Notes

1. Beth Wohlford, "No Compromise," from Sunday bulletin of Willow Creek Community Church, 27 August, 1995, p. 5.
2. C.W. Christian, "My Faith Is Small," *Moonlight and Stuff,* self-published, 1990. Used by permission.

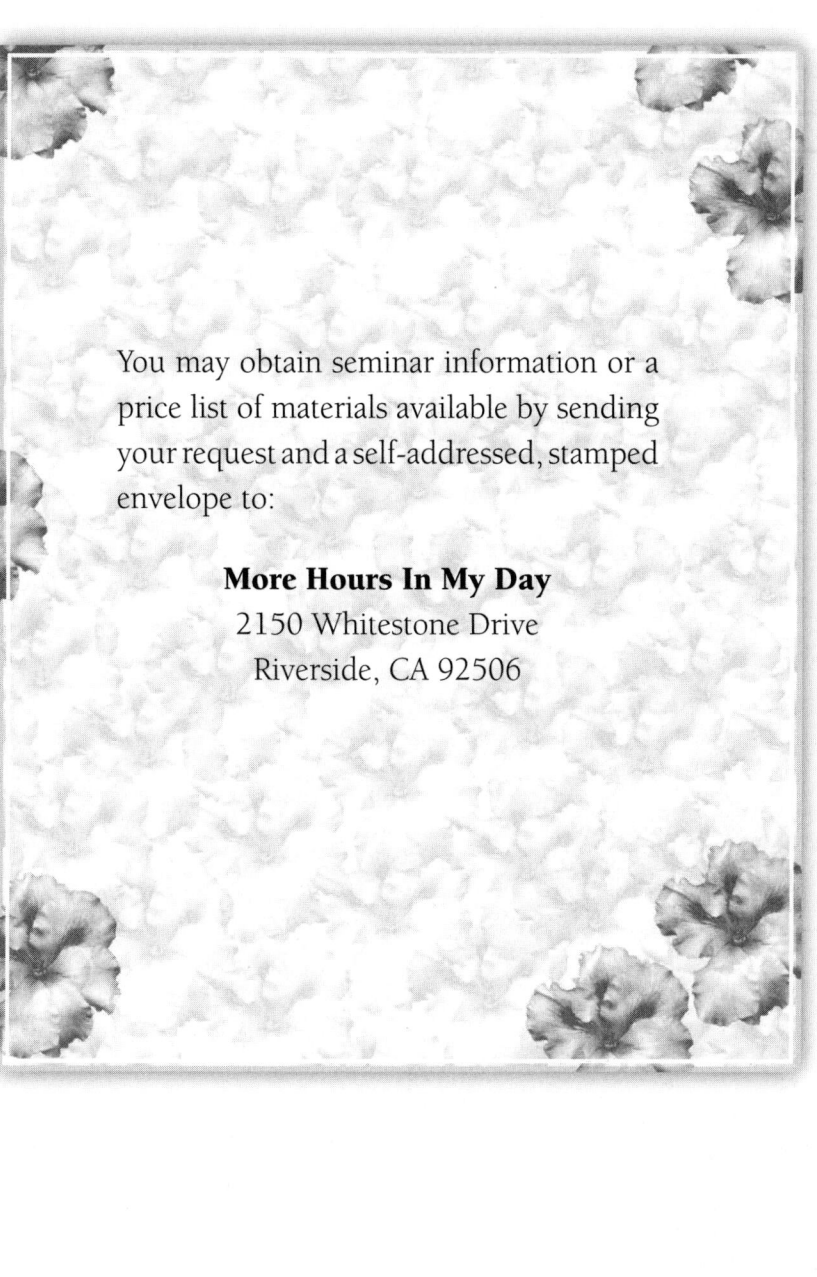

You may obtain seminar information or a price list of materials available by sending your request and a self-addressed, stamped envelope to:

More Hours In My Day
2150 Whitestone Drive
Riverside, CA 92506

Harvest House Books by Bob & Emilie Barnes

Bob & Emilie Barnes

*15-Minute Devotions
for Couples*
101 Ways to Love Your Grandkids
Be My Refuge, Lord
*A Little Book of Manners
for Boys*
*Minute Meditations
for Couples*

Bob Barnes

*15 Minutes Alone
with God for Men*
*500 Handy Hints for
Every Husband*
Men Under Construction
*What Makes a Man
Feel Loved*

Emilie Barnes

The 15-Minute Organizer
15 Minutes Alone with God
*15 Minutes of Peace
with God*
*15 Minutes with God
for Grandma*
*500 Time-Saving Hints
for Women*
Cleaning Up the Clutter
Designing Your Home on a Budget
*Emilie's Creative
Home Organizer*
*Everything I Know
I Learned in My Garden*
*Everything I Know
I Learned over Tea*
Friendship Teas to Go

Garden Moment Getaways
A Grandma Is a Gift from God
Heal My Heart, Lord
Home Warming
If Teacups Could Talk
I Need Your Strength, Lord
An Invitation to Tea
Join Me for Tea
Journey Through Cancer
*Keep It Simple
for Busy Women*
Let's Have a Tea Party!
A Little Book of Manners
A Little Hero in the Making
A Little Princess in the Making
Meet Me Where I Am, Lord
*Minute Meditations
for Busy Moms*
*Minute Meditations for Healing
and Hope*
More Faith in My Day
More Hours in My Day
One-Minute Home Organizer
*Quiet Moments for
a Busy Mom's Soul*
A Quiet Refuge
Safe in the Father's Hands
*Simple Secrets to
a Beautiful Home*
Survival for Busy Moms
A Tea to Comfort Your Soul
*The Twelve Teas®
of Celebration*
*The Twelve Teas®
of Friendship*
The Twelve Teas® of Inspiration
What Makes a Woman Feel Loved